in their own words

the Beatles
...*after the* break-up

David Bennahum

OMNIBUS PRESS
LONDON · NEW YORK · SYDNEY

Edited by Chris Charlesworth
Cover designed by Pearce Marchbank
Book designed by Pete Dolton
Picture research by Dave Brolan

ISBN 0 7119 2558 5
Order No OP 46424

Exclusive Distributors:

Music Sales Corporation
257 Park Avenue South,
New York, NY 10010

Music Sales Limited
8/9 Frith Street
London W1V 5TZ England

Music Sales Pty. Limited
120 Rothschild Street
Rosebery, Sydney, NSW 2018, Australia

To the Music Trade only:

Music Sales Limited
8/9 Frith Street
London W1V 5TZ England

Printed in the United States of America by
Vicks Lithograph and Printing

PICTURE CREDITS

Associated Press: 20(b), 65; Tony Bramwell: 14; Camera Press: 121; Richard Dilello: 19, 49, 52(t), 104; Ian Forsyth:
54; London Features International: 4(t&b), 9, 10, 11, 12, 13, 17, 18, 20, 22, 28(t&b), 29, 30, 31, 32, 35(t), 36,
40(t&b), 41, 42, 43, 50, 53, 55, 60, 62, 72, 76, 77, 82, 84, 86, 87(l), 88, 90, 91, 92, 95, 97, 98, 100, 103, 105, 106,
108, 109, 110, 113, 115, 118, 119, 123, 125; Pictorial Press: 5(t&b), 8, 15, 16, 21, 25, 38, 44, 48(l), 51, 56, 58, 59,
66, 67, 70, 71, 75, 78, 81, 96, 102, 107, 111, 112, 116, 117, 122, 126; Rex Features: 23, 24, 27, 33, 34, 37, 39, 45,
46, 47, 48(r), 52(b), 61, 63, 64, 68, 73, 74, 85, 89, 94, 99, 101, 114, 120; Syndication International: 80.

CONTENTS

Introduction

Perspective only comes with time. What do The Beatles mean to the ex-fab four? What effect did being a Beatle have on the life and solo careers of John, Paul, George and Ringo? With quotes ranging from 1970 to the 1990s, the former Beatles give an intimate portrait of what it was like leaving The Beatles and developing separate lives.

In 1970, Paul left The Beatles determined to establish his own identity as an independent performer. Paul's new band, Wings, made a point of drawing a line

between The Beatles and the present. In 1977, Paul released a single, 'Mull Of Kintyre', that outsold any Beatles' single. Symbolically, this proved to the world that Paul didn't need The Beatles to be a success. Paul then disbanded Wings, stopped touring, devoted himself to the studio and expanded a business empire. With time, Paul slowly accepted and rediscovered his past with The Beatles. Through the 1980s Paul shared with the world his thoughts on The Beatles, his solo career and what John meant to him. In 1990 Paul took to the road again, shattering concert attendance records world-wide. Paul had come full circle since 1970, revelling in his Beatle heritage and playing many Beatles classics never before played in public.

George left The Beatles to pursue what was initially the most successful solo career of the four. Free from the constraints of The Beatles, George could fully develop his

musical style. However, by the mid-1970s, George lost interest in touring and turned inward, focusing on family and religion. Like Paul, George developed a keen business acumen and formed a film company, Hand Made Films, which teamed up with members of the Monty Python team to produce the controversial *Life of Brian*. George went on to produce mainstream box-office hits and alternative films acclaimed around the world for their quality. In 1988, George reappeared on the music scene with a hit album, *Cloud Nine*. He too had come to terms with his Beatle past and

celebrated it in songs like 'When We Were Fab' and 'All Those Years Ago'. Rediscovering the vitality of performance, George then joined a studio band, The Traveling Wilburys, with his friends Bob Dylan, Tom Petty, Jeff Lynne and the late Roy Orbison.

Ringo left The Beatles and surprised everyone in the early 1970s with his recording success. Of the four, Ringo came closest to bringing the ex-Beatles together, John,

Paul and George all contributed to his 1973 hit album 'Ringo'. But as the 1980s arrived, Ringo gracefully faded into obscurity, only to reappear from time to time in the social pages, as a talk-show guest and a narrator on children's television. The only former Beatle to appear in advertisements, Ringo promoted a brand of vodka in the U.S. However, in 1989 a remarkable transformation occurred. Overcoming his alcohol and drug dependency, Ringo formed a band, Ringo's All-Starrs, and toured America with success. Today, Ringo is once again active as a performer and has rediscovered the love of his life, the drums.

From 1970 to 1975 John, as with the other ex-Beatles, struggled to develop and discover an identity outside of The Beatles. Never one to shy away from controversy, John constantly pushed the limits of the conventional or acceptable in his music and

art. His early solo work stunned critics and was immensely popular with the public. John maintained his flair for coining universal one-liners, notably 'Give Peace A Chance', which remains the global anthem for peace activists throughout the world. Then, after teetering on the edge of self-destruction, John disappeared from the public eye for nearly five years to sort out his affairs and look after his young son Sean. His intense artistic energy nearly consumed him, but John pulled back from the brink to re-establish his identity. By 1980 John felt ready and excited

to create artistically once again. His murder cut short whatever possibilities this artistic renaissance held for the world.

This book gives an intimate portrait of the on-again off-again relationship between John, Paul, George and Ringo. It covers all aspects of their life and work since the breakup. As we all know, The Beatles' story didn't end in 1970. It continues to this day.

David Bennahum

ACKNOWLEDGEMENTS

The author would like to thank the following people and organizations for their assistance. The British Newspaper Library in Colindale, London. Chris Charlesworth, Dave Brolan and the rest of the Omnibus staff; Music Sales. And a very special thanks to Bob Wise for giving me this opportunity.

David Bennahum

"You say goodbye and I say hello..."

The Break Up

After Brian (Epstein) died we collapsed. Paul took over and supposedly led us. But what is leading us when we went round in circles? We broke up then. That was the disintegration. John, 1970

No matter how much we split, we're still very linked. We're the only four people who've seen the whole Beatlemania bit from the inside out, so we're tied forever, whatever happens. **Paul, April 1970**

I didn't leave The Beatles. The Beatles have left The Beatles but no one wants to be the one to say the party's over. **Paul, 1970**

'Wedding Bells' is what it was: "Wedding bells are breaking up that old gang of mine". We used to sing that song...It was like an army song and for us The Beatles became the army. We always knew that one day 'Wedding Bells' would come true, and that was when it did. **Paul, October 1986**

The actual story in my mind is that it was all getting a bit sticky during the 'White Album'. And 'Let It Be' was very sticky – George left the group then, and so did Ringo, but we managed to patch that back up. The dates are all purple haze to me, but at some point – after 'Let It Be' was finished, and about the time I was wanting to put the 'McCartney' album out – we had a

meeting at the Apple office, and it was like, "Look, something's wrong and we've got to sort it out." I had my suggestion: I said, "What I think we ought to do is get back as a band – get back as the little unit we always were. I think we ought to hit small clubs and do a little tour." I just wanted to learn to be a band together again, 'cause we'd become a business group. We'd become businessmen. So that was my big suggestion.   And John looked me in the eye and he said, "I think you're daft. In fact, I wasn't gonna tell you...but I'm leavin' the group." To my recollection, those were his exact words. And our jaws dropped. And then he went on to explain that it was rather a good feelin' to get it off his chest – a bit like when he told his wife (Cynthia) about a divorce, that he'd had a sort of feeling of relief. Which was very nice for him, but we didn't get much of a good feeling.

At first we agreed not to announce it. But after three or four months, I got more and more guilty about people saying, "How's the group going?" when we sort of knew it was probably split up. So I did a kind of dumb move in the end, and when I look back on it, it was really...it looks very hard and cold. But I was releasing the 'McCartney' album, and I didn't really want to do much press for it; so I told a guy from the office to do me a list of questions and I'll write the answers and we'll print it up as a pamphlet and just stick it in with the press copies of the album . The questions were quite pointed, and it ended up being like me announcing that The Beatles had broken up. John got quite mad about that, apparently – this is one of the things he said really hurt him and cut him to the quick. Personally, I don't think it was such a bad thing to announce to the world after four months that we'd broken up. It had to come out sometime. I think maybe the manner of doing it I regret now – I wish it had been a little kinder, or with the others' approval. But I felt it was time.
Paul, January 1986

We didn't accept Yoko totally, but how many groups do you know who would? It's a joke, like *Spinal Tap*. You know, I loved John, I was his best mate for a long time. Then the group started to break up. It was very sad. I got the rap as the guy who broke the group up. It wasn't actually true.
Paul, October 1986

When I was in The Beatles I could never understand when they said: "What are you going to do when the bubble bursts?" It was a joke question. We always used to say, "We'll burst with it – ha, ha."

It was the only thing we could think of, just to answer the thing. But I never took it in. I never understood what they meant. What does it mean, "when the bubble bursts, I'll be dead?" When it bursts, I'll be dead. Never understood the question really. I never took it in until The Beatles broke up. And they were always going on about "the pressures." I could see there were pressures. I couldn't feel them! I was just a rocker...I didn't begin to feel any until the big, dramatic breakup of The Beatles. **Paul, 1984**

It's just like divorce. It's that you were so close and so in love that if anyone decides to start talking dirty – great, then Pandora's box is open. That's what happened with us. **Paul, November 1987**

Immediately after the breakup of The Beatles I felt, "What am I gonna do?" I then went into a period when everybody started to call me a hermit in isolation...I was trying to get normal again, and giving myself time to think, what do I want to do? **Paul, 1984**

When The Beatles split up, I fell on the rocks. I've been accused of walking out on them but I never did. It's something I'd never do. One day John left and that was the last straw. It was the signal for the others to leave. The Beatles were a blanket of security. When the job folded beneath me, suddenly I didn't have a career any more. I wasn't earning anything. All my money was in Apple. I couldn't get it because I'd signed it all away. I stayed up all night drinking and smoking and watching TV. I lost all my security. I had no idea what to do, there seemed no point in me joining another group. **Paul, 1984**

Shooting the 'Abbey Road' sleeve outside the studios in St John's Wood, London.

There was a certain amount of relief after that Candlestick Park concert. Before one of the last numbers, we actually set up this camera – I think it had a fisheye, a very wide-angle lens. We set it up on the amplifier and Ringo came off the drums, and we stood with our backs to the audience and posed for a photograph, because we knew that was the last show.

There was a sense of relief after that, getting home. Then we spent what seemed like fifty years going in and out of each other's houses, writing tunes and going into the studio for 'Sgt. Pepper' and the 'White Album'. But for me, I think for all of us, it was just too much. The novelty had worn off. Everybody was growing up. Everybody was getting married and leaving home, in effect, I think it was inevitable really. **George, November 1987**

I realise The Beatles did fill a space in the '60s and all the people The Beatles meant something to have grown up. It's like with anything. You grow up with it and you get attached to things. That's one of the problems in our lives, becoming attached to things, and it's appreciated that people still like them.

Showing off their MBEs, 1965.

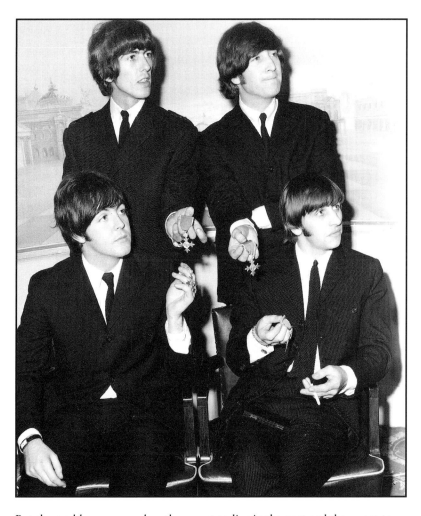

But the problem comes when they want to live in the past and they want to hold on to something and are afraid to change. **George, 1974**

All this stuff about The Beatles being able to save the world was rubbish. I can't even save myself. It was just people trying to put the responsibility on our shoulders. The thing about The Beatles is that they saved the world from boredom...But we didn't really create any great change, we just heralded that change of consciousness that happened in the sixties. We went along with it, that's all. The whole Beatles thing is a nightmare. I don't even like to talk about it. I just hate it. **George, 1983**

Beatle producer, George Martin, said recently how he always felt sorry because he concentrated more on them and he should have paid more attention to me. He said, "I hope you'll forgive me." But I'm quite happy with my role in The Beatles. You know, it split up because of all those problems, there were too many songs. Because we got too close to each other, but I'm quite happy about the way things went. I feel that whatever I am now, I always have been that, you know. Maybe different things have taken longer to reach the surface or whatever, but I'm who I am and I am not really that much different to how I was then. Maybe I'm more able to express it or maybe people are more interested now in what I have to say. Because in the sixties and the early seventies they thought I was a loony. **George, 1988**

I think being (a Beatle) was much more difficult. I mean, it was fun for a long time, but there was so much pressure on us. It became really tiresome and it was good, in a way, to dissipate that energy that there was with the four of us together. You know, let it go away so that we could have some semblance of a life. Otherwise it would have just been madness continually. **George, 1988**

Even now I look back and I can see, relative to a lot of other groups or pop music in general, The Beatles did have something. But that's relative to that. Relative to something else...I can accept whatever The Beatles were on those terms. But it's a bit too much to accept that we're supposedly the designers of this incredible change that occurred (in the '60s). In many ways we were just swept along with everybody else. **George, November 1987**

Yes, I was in The Beatles. Yes, we made some great records together. Yes, I love those boys. But that's the end of the story. **Ringo, 1978**

Things were getting a bit rough, and I'd left The Beatles for a couple of weeks because I couldn't take it any more. So I went on holiday with my family to Sardinia. A friend lent us a boat, and one day the captain served us some octopus for lunch. Naturally we all went, "Urrgghh-ah! No thanks. Have you got any egg and chips?" But I started talking to the captain, and he told me all about octopuses, how they go 'round the sea-bed and pick up stones and shiny objects and build gardens. I thought, "How fabulous!" 'cause at the time, I just wanted to get out of (The Beatles) for a while. Of course, I ended up going back to the group because I couldn't play with anyone better. But that's how 'Octopus' Garden' came about. **Ringo, April 1981**

Yoko's taken a lot of shit, her and Linda (McCartney); but The Beatles break-up wasn't their fault. It was just that suddenly we were all thirty and married and changed. We couldn't carry on that life any more. **Ringo, 1981**

I'm not sorry I went through it (Beatlemania), but that was then, and we had a lot of good times, but I don't really ever want to do it again. I don't want to go on the road again; I enjoy the studios more now. **Ringo, January 1974**

The '60s was totally different. I mean, that was the fabs up there, this was just the greats (Ringo's All-Starr Band tour of 1989). It was a zoo attitude. They just came to see you, no one could hear anything. By 1965 we were turning into such bad musicians 'cos we were just playing chords on the beat. There was no groove to it, and that's why we stopped (touring).
Ringo, January 1991

On The Beatles' Enduring Fame: Well, who else is there? There's nobody else. You couldn't have "Elton John Week" – even though Reg is a very nice lad, when he wants to be. They do Elvis and they do us. Everyone can relate to The Beatles, you know, children who weren't born relate through the music.

We always did songs which related to everybody from children to our parents and grandparents. And now we're the parents and my mother is a grandparent and she still relates. I mean, the melody lingers on – everyone relates to 'Yesterday' and half the people still relate to "I Am The Walrus." We were the monsters. There's been a lot of biggies, and very few monsters. That's the difference. **Ringo, 1976**

Proof of The Beatles' Demise: The Beatles' 'White Album'. Listen – all you experts listen, none of you can hear. Every track is an individual track – there isn't any Beatle music on it. I just say, listen to the 'White Album'. It was John and the Band, Paul and the Band, George and the Band, like that. What I did was sort of say, "Fuck the band. I'll make John – I'll do it with Yoko," or whatever. I put four albums out last year (1969) and I didn't say a fucking word about quitting. **John, May 1970**

On Quitting The Beatles First: Well, I said to Paul, "I'm leaving." We were in Apple, and...I knew before we went to Toronto. I told Allen (Klein) I was leaving, I told Eric Clapton and Klaus (Voorman) that I was leaving and that I'd like to probably use them as a group. I hadn't decided how to do it – to have a permanent new group or what, then later on I thought, fuck, I'm not going to get stuck with another set of people around me on the way to Toronto a few days before. And on the plane, Allen came to me, and I told Allen it's over. When I got back there were a few meetings and Allen had said, "Well, cool it, cool it," 'cause there was a lot to do businesswise, you know, and it would not have been suitable at the time.

And then we were discussing something in the office with Paul and Paul

said something or other like we ought to do something and I kept saying no, no, no to everything he said, you see. So it came to a point I had to say something, of course, and Paul said, "What do you mean?" I said, "I mean the group is over. I'm leaving."

Allen was saying don't tell. He didn't want me to tell Paul even. Well, I couldn't help it, so I said it out, I couldn't stop it, it came out. Paul and Allen said they were glad that I wasn't going to announce it. Like I was going to

make an event out of it. But Paul and Allen both...I don't know whether Paul said don't tell anybody but he was damn pleased that I wasn't, you know. He said, "Oh, well, that means nothing really happened if you're not going to say anything."

So, like anybody when you say divorce, you know, their face goes all sorts of colours. It's like he knew, really, that this was the final thing. And then six months later he comes out with whatever. A lot of people knew I left. I was a fool not to do it, not to do what Paul did, which use it to sell a record ('McCartney'). **John, 1970**

You know, it's like this, when we read all this shit (about the breakup) in the paper, Yoko and I were laughing because the cartoon is this: four guys on a stage with a spotlight on them; second picture, three guys onstage, breezing out of the spotlight; third picture, one guy standing there, shouting, "I'm leaving." We were all out of it. **John, May 1970**

One has to completely humiliate oneself to be what The Beatles were, and that's what I resent. I mean I did it, I didn't know, I didn't foresee; it just happened bit by bit, gradually, until this complete craziness is surrounding you and you're doing exactly what you don't want to do with people you can't stand, the people you hated when you were ten. **John, 1970**

LEFT: John, during the recording of the 'White' album.

Fuckin' big bastards, that's what The Beatles were. You have to be a bastard to make it, and that's a fact. And The Beatles are the biggest bastards on earth. **John, 1970**

I don't believe in The Beatles, that's all. I don't believe in The Beatles myth. "I don't believe in The Beatles" – there is no other way of saying it, is there? I don't believe in them whatever they were supposed to be in everybody's head, including our own heads for a period. It was a dream. I don't believe in the dream any more. **John, 1970**

You see we believed The Beatles myth, too. I don't know whether the others still believe it. We were four guys...I met Paul and said, "You want to join the band?" you know. Then George joined and Ringo joined. We were just a band who made it very, very big, that's all. Our best work was never

George, John and Paul in Hamburg.

recorded...Because we were performers – in spite of what Mick (Jagger) says about us – in Liverpool, Hamburg and other dance halls what we generated was fantastic, where we played straight rock, and there was nobody to touch us in Britain. As soon as we made it, we made it, but the edges were knocked off. Brian (Epstein) put us in suits and all that and we made it very, very big. But we sold out, you know. The music was dead before we even went on the theatre tour of Britain. **John, 1970**

"You never give me your money..."

Business & Money

Yoko, John and Paul launch Apple.

I advise anybody who has written a song to own it themselves. But no publisher will let you own the copyright. I always harp on about 'Yesterday' because it's a big song of mine, the only big one that I did on my own. I don't own the copyright of that. Paul, 1984

I'm not very into luxury. I'm not very impressed with it really. I think luxury is a transition phase between not having much money and having a bit of money.

The example that always sums it up for me was John, when we first all got loaded, he moved out to Weybridge, very near a golf club and it was very much the landed gentry kind of thing. And you could have anything you wanted, kind of, in the first flush of success. He went mad on Jaffa Cakes! He went insane about them, gimme gimme gimme. And about a week later he couldn't look at one. For the rest of his life it was, "Don't talk to me about Jaffa Cakes." **Paul, July 1989**

The thing is, you've got to remember when I first got money with The Beatles, it's quite a long time ago, so I've had a lot of time to adjust and to pace myself, and get sensible with it all. And this is what I think is a sensible way to live with money, which is not to have it rule you but really take full advantage of it. **Paul, July 1989**

Paul appearing on Juke Box Jury.

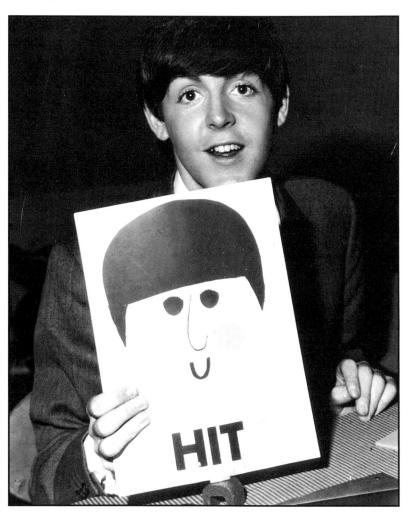

We used to ask (the accountants), "Am I a millionaire yet?" and they used to say cryptic things like, "On paper you are." And we'd say, "Well, what does that mean? Am I or aren't I? Are there more than a million of those green things in my bank yet?" and they'd say, "Well, it's not actually in a bank...we think you are." It was actually very difficult to get anything out of these people and the accountants never made you feel successful.
Paul, October 1986

Somebody said to me, "But The Beatles were anti-materialistic." That's a huge myth, John and I literally used to sit down and say, "Now let's write a swimming pool." We said it out of innocence. Out of normal fucking working-class glee that we were able to write a swimming pool. For the first time in our lives, we could actually do something and earn money.
Paul, February 1990

We were always cheated, and I don't care who likes or dislikes that statement. From the word go, our songs were always "Lennon-McCartney." That could have been altered somewhere along the line, but it never was. So even a totally self-written song like 'Yesterday', which John had nothing to do with – only I played on the record, it was me and a string quartet – then you start to think, "Well, maybe I've got a tiny right to...something." Civil rights, maybe, or...human rights? Isn't there one piddling little right I can claim? But there isn't. I don't have any rights whatsoever. I just get a tip. But I get a handsome tip and I have to be happy with that. **Paul, November 1987**

Paul and I made a deal when we were 15. There was never a legal deal between us, just a deal we made when we decided to write together that we put both our names on it, no matter what. **John, September 1980**

John's (copyright) renewals will be coming up, and Yoko can get the rights back. But my renewals don't come up, because I'm still alive and we signed our renewal rights away for life. So, pretty soon, I think Yoko will own more of 'Yesterday' than I will. Like, what can I say? All I can say is, "You'll have more of our (Lennon-McCartney) songs than I do pretty soon." The reason I mentioned 'Yesterday' is because I wrote that song, but it was our deal that we'd split everything down the middle. So that is one particular case in point and it just happens to be the most covered song in history.

But you know what? Having said all this – it's great to get it off my chest – I really don't care, I've done great, and it's just churlish to...I mean, it niggles a little bit, but generally I just think, "Aw come on, I was part of this fabulous thing. I wrote those things. I was there with John while we did them all." So what the hell, I gave a bit too much of it away. Big deal. I can live with that and still sleep at night. **Paul, November 1987**

I had to take the other Beatles to court. And I got a lot of guilt off that. But you tell me what you would have done if the entire earnings that you'd made – and it was something like The Beatles' entire earnings, a big figure, everything we'd ever done up to somewhere round about 'Hey Jude' – was about to disappear into someone's pocket. The guy I'm talking about, Allen Klein, had £5 million the first year he managed The Beatles. So I smelled a rat and thought, £5 million in one year, how long is it going to take him to get rid of it all?

And I said, "Well, I want out of this. I want to sue this guy Klein." They said, "You can't, because he's not party to any of the agreements." So it became clear that I had to sue The Beatles. So obviously I became the baddie. I did take The Beatles to the High Court, which was a highly traumatic period for me, having to front that one out. Imagine, seriously, having to front that one out. **Paul, October 1986**

I hate that thing "business differences." You know Apple still isn't sorted out, it's only 20 years later (since the breakup). We've all got our sides to the story; my story is that I just want us to divide it in four and go home. And then be nice to each other. But all our advisers say it's not as simple as that, so it goes on forever. **Paul, July 1989**

Why Paul Didn't Go With George and Ringo to Accept The Beatles' Induction Into The Rock & Roll Hall of Fame: I keep saying to everyone, "We've got to sort out our problems. We can't move forward in harmony while you're suing me." So I wanted that to be the reunion night, and I said, "If you can drop this lawsuit guys, or just nearly drop it, show me something that says you love me, give me a sign, a wink." And it just went and went, I kept ringing. George was in Hawaii. I got a message back from him, "Sit tight, don't rock the boat, don't worry." But that wasn't good enough. So I had to ring him up and say I couldn't go to the Rock & Roll Hall of Fame, no way was I standing up on stage going, "Yo! United!" when I know they're suing me. I just couldn't do it. **Paul, July 1989**

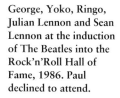

George, Yoko, Ringo, Julian Lennon and Sean Lennon at the induction of The Beatles into the Rock'n'Roll Hall of Fame, 1986. Paul declined to attend.

I'm starting to get back with (George and Ringo). It's all business troubles. If we don't talk about Apple then we get on like a house on fire. So I've just started to see them again. **Paul, October 1986**

On Michael Jackson Buying the Rights to The Beatles' Songs: I gave him a lot of advice, and you know, a fish gets caught by opening its mouth. I advised him to go into publishing. And as a joke he looked at me and he said, "I'm going to buy your songs one day." And I just said, "Great, good joke." I really treated it as a joke. And I just couldn't believe it, you know, someone rang me up one day and said, "Michael's bought your..." "What?!?"

So, you know, I haven't spoken to him since. I think he thinks it's just business. I think it's slightly dodgy to do things like that – to be someone's friend and then to buy the rug they're standing on. **Paul, November 1987**

Artistry and Record Sales: You've got sales. That's why I always feel it's funny when people say, "Oh, it doesn't matter whether it sells, you don't look at that aspect." I think that's what does matter, the people out there with their little pennies, going to the shop and spending them. I think that's a big move, to spend your money on someone. So that's what I tend to look at, if people will buy it. Some people think that's just commercialism, but I think it's the public vote. **Paul, July 1989**

The Music Business Today: Well, it's totally different, really. In those days, it was the four of us. We just went into the studios and made some records, went out for a tour, then went back in the studio to make some more records. That was it really. Nowadays, it's a big business and it has to be coordinated. With The Beatles, after around 1964, we just had to put the records out and people rushed out to buy them. It's not like that these days. You have to work with the record labels and coordinate releases and do a lot of promotion work. I'm on my own, whereas in the past I had three other smartasses with me all cracking jokes. **George, 1988**

It's one thing writing a song, taping it and then making a record, but I wasn't interested in promoting myself after all that had happened with The Beatles. I'm not into myself in that manner, and I think you have to be quite a bit of an egomaniac to go touring and promoting yourself all the time. There was a bit of pressure once I got started making my own records, because everyone expected each of us to be as powerful as The Beatles, which was an impossibility.

Sometimes, you release an album and the record company just about ignores it, and so many people don't even know it's out. And I'm not about to jump up and down shouting, "Hey folks, look at me! I'm cool and groovy!" That's not what George Harrison is all about. **George, 1988**

I got a bit tired of (the music industry) back around about 1980. I just felt there was no point. The way the music was going, I couldn't relate to it. I just thought, "Well, I've got a lot of other things to do, so I might as well have a rest." Nowadays, I never consider that I'm going to be out there with this

George supports a
'Nuclear Freeze', 1986.

record and people may not buy it or whatever. I didn't even think about that. I mean, if you have a flop, it's a flop. I think you have to just make something that you enjoy yourself and see what happens. And I've had enough success in my life that if I fail, it's okay. **George, 1988**

Plagiarism and Music Copyrights: I'd be willing every time I write a song if somebody will have a computer and I can just go up to the thing and sing my new song into it and the computer will say "sorry" or "yes, ok." I'm willing to do that, because the last thing I want to do is keep spending the rest of my life in court, or being faced with people thinking, "Oh, well, they beat Harrison on 'My Sweet Lord', let's sue"...they can sue the world! It made me so paranoid about writing. And I thought, "God, I don't even want to touch the guitar or the piano, in case I'm touching somebody's note." Somebody might own that note, so you'd better watch out. **George, 1983**

(George) walked right into it. He knew what he was doing...He's smarter than that. It's irrelevant, actually – only on a monetary level does it matter. He could have changed a couple of bars in that song and nobody could have touched him, but he just let it go and paid the price. **John, September 1980**

George Creates Hand Made Films: Well, I've just been friendly with (Monty Python) for a long time and when they were beginning *Life Of Brian*, the original film company backed out as they were right into post-production. A friend of mine asked if I could think of any way to help. I asked my business manager and he thought about it for a few days, then he came back and he said, "Yeah, okay, we'll be the producers." So we borrowed the money from the bank and formed Hand Made Films. I did it because I wanted to see the film. I couldn't stand the idea of it not being made. **George, 1988**

I hate business and all that wheeling and dealing...I go to the set and I'm meant to be the big cheese, but I'm not really. Making films is sort of a hobby for me. I can't let it become too serious, otherwise it'd become work. And once I'd got myself out of that star rat-race, I promised myself I'd never work again. Well, I do work, but I want it to be enjoyable, not just a slog.

We make the sort of films that I went to see, which means we pick up a lot of films the other companies don't want. We're not looking for enormous success: we're just lads mucking about making interesting films that wouldn't normally get made. You see, you've got to take chances to make something worthwhile. **George, 1979**

George After Hand Made Films' *Mona Lisa* Won the Best-Actor Award at the Cannes Film Festival: In the midst of all these *Rambo*-type films that are just crash, bang, wallop, there's a shortage of films that touch the human side. Although *Mona Lisa* is about the seedy side of life, it's funny, and the characters are very real. It allows the audience to use their intelligence. That's pretty rare; most of those American films treat the audience as if they were idiots. **George, 1986**

Ringo Runs a Company: I realised that to run the company you've got to come to the office every day, which I did. And you've got to go and have all those meetings, which I hated, because you'd have all these meetings and nothing would happen. You usually have meetings to decide about the next meeting. So I did tend to leave it alone – and then I just decided I didn't want it no more: "I'm getting out of here..." **Ringo, 1979**

Ringo and George at the Prince's Trust Concert, Wembley Arena, 1987.

Ringo and the Failure of Ring O' Records: I think we had some good artists, but maybe we were the only ones who thought they were any good. Well, the people outside didn't think they were that terrific because they didn't buy their records and that is what a record company is all about. If you don't sell records, then it costs you money. So when it costs you a certain amount of money, you have to look it straight and say: "What's going on." And you either turn it around or you do as I did and decide, yet again, that it's time for it to end. **Ringo, 1979**

Ringo Loses his Polydor Record Contract: The record company is not going to control my artistic life. I can give them the records and they can sell them if they can. They kept asking me to do these shows all over the world, but at that point I didn't want to do it. I just didn't want to get into that situation. **Ringo, 1979**

Being Rich and Being Ringo: Well, I am a jet-setter. Whatever anyone may think and whoever puts it down, I am on planes half the year going to different places. And, in people's eyes, Monte Carlo is a jet-set scene. Los Angeles is a jet-set scene. London – swinging London, not that it swings any more. Amsterdam, you know. It's a crazy kind of world. Wherever I go, it's a swinging place, man.

I like the position I'm in where I can do what I want to do. But, of course, occasionally, they force me to work and then, occasionally, I force everyone else to work. When I want to do something, I have my little tantrums when I say, "Why don't we do this?" And they all go, "Oh, God, he's off again..." **Ringo, 1979**

In England, there are only two things to be, basically: you are either for the labour movement or for the capitalist movement. Either you become a right-wing Archie Bunker if you are in the class I am in, or you become an instinctive socialist, which I was. That meant I think people should get their false teeth and their health looked after, all the rest of it. But apart from that, I worked for money and I wanted to be rich. So what the hell – if that's a paradox, then I'm a socialist. But I am not anything. What I used to be is guilty about money. That's why I lost it, either by giving it away or by allowing myself to be screwed by so-called managers. **John, September 1980**

I always felt bad that George and Ringo didn't get a piece of the publishing. When the opportunity came to give them five percent each of MacLen, it was because of me they got it. It was not because of Klein and not because of Paul but because of me. **John, September 1980**

How do you describe the job, you know, my job...I manoeuvre people, that's what leaders do. And I sit and make situations which will be of benefit to me with other people. It's as simple as that. I'm manoeuvred too. I had to do a job to get Allen (Klein) in Apple. I did a job, so did you.

Manoeuvering is what it is. Let's not be coy about it. It's a deliberate and thought-out manoeuvre of how to get a situation how we want it. That's what life's about, isn't it. It is not? Isn't it? **John, 1970**

The Male Establishment and Yoko: They can't stand it. But they have to stand it, because (Yoko) is who represents us. They're all male, you know, just big and fat, vodka lunch, shouting males, like trained dogs, trained to attack all the time. **John, September 1980**

Money can't buy me love: Allen Klein with John and Yoko at the Apple HQ.

Recently, (Yoko) made it possible for us to earn a large sum of money that benefited all of them and they fought and fought not to let her do it, because it was her idea and she was a woman and she was not a professional. But she did it, and then one of the guys said to her, "Well, Lennon does it again." But Lennon didn't have anything to do with it. **John, September 1980**

Money and Morality: What would you suggest I do? Give everything away and walk the streets? The Buddhist says, "Get rid of the possessions of the mind." Walking away from all the money would not accomplish that.
John, September 1980

Allen Klein.

We (John & Yoko) tried to put ('John Lennon: Plastic Ono Band') out on Capitol, and Capitol didn't want to put it out. They said, "This is garbage; we're not going to put it out with her screaming on one side and you doing this sort of live stuff." And they just refused to put it out. But we finally persuaded them that, you know, people might buy this. Of course it went gold the next day. And then the funny thing was – this is a side story – (Allen) Klein had got a deal on that record that it was a John and Yoko Plastic Ono record, not a Beatles record, so we could get a higher royalty, because The Beatles' royalties were so low; they'd been locked up in '63 – and Capitol said, "Sure you can have it, you know. Nobody's going to buy that crap." They just threw it away and gave it to us. And it came out, and it was fairly successful and it went gold. I don't know what chart position, but I've got a gold record somewhere that says...And four years later, we go to collect the royalties, and you know what they say? "This is a Beatle record." So Capitol has it under my file under Beatles records. Isn't it incredible?
John, December 6, 1980

You see, the point about me cooking and (Yoko) doing the business, before we'd always had somebody come in to look after the business, and, you know the story of that. Some lawyer or accountant would come in and say, "I'll handle it all for you." Since 1962 they'd been handling it, and there's been nothing but tax problems and, you know, whatever. For a long history of it. Like we don't own any of The Beatles' songs, we don't own any of The Beatles' records, we've got farthings for royalties and all the rest of it. Anyway, the point being, we decided not to have an outside party. We had to look after our own stuff and face that reality. (Yoko) could deal with it, so I could go to the other side which I could deal with. I'm a homebody, I always like to hang around the house. **John, December 6, 1980**

Sean and I were away for a weekend and Yoko came over to sell this cow and I was joking about it. We hadn't seen her for days; she spent all her time on it. But then I read the paper that said she sold it for a quarter of a million dollars. Only Yoko could sell a cow for that much. **John, September 1980**

I was terrified. I was saying can we put ('Double Fantasy') out without, without putting it out? Couldn't we do something else? Do I have to put my name on the paper?...Since 1962 I was signed up to somebody or other, and thankful to be in 1962, but what you sing when you are 21 and it goes on for 20 years and they all own you, life and soul and you can never get out of it. So I liked the five years when all contracts were free. I was free of any contractual obligation when (Yoko) finally says, "Look you're going to have to sign something to say that they have the right to put the record ('Double Fantasy') out." I was saying, "Are you sure? You're sure? Why don't you sign it? You figure it, I don't want to put me name on it," but we made arrangements which didn't make me feel paranoid because I don't want to owe people nothing. I don't want to...the point of being a musician or artist to me was the freedom. **John, December 6, 1980**

"I never needed anybody's help in any way..."

Solo Work

Ringo in *That'll Be The Day*.

Well there are career moves, and there are things you just want to do. Most of the time I do things 'cause I just want to do them, which isn't necessarily right, but you know, I like to have a good time! Ringo, 1981

I'm not coming back. I'm starting all over again and working my way upwards. It's like boxing. You don't fight Cassius Clay on your first time out. A year ago I used to wake up in the morning and think, "I'm a myth. I'm Paul McCartney." And it scared the hell out of me. **Paul, 1973**

Don't ever call me ex-Beatle McCartney again. That was a band I was with. Now I'm not with them. Now I've got another band. We're not bothered with trying to please the people ALL the time. All we want with Wings is to please ourselves with our music. I get irritated by people constantly harping on about the past, about the days when I was with that other band. The Beatles were my old job. We're not friends. We just know each other. **Paul, November 1972**

Paul on his Music After The Beatles: What I like about the music I've written in that period is, I kind of think it's undiscovered: it's really just been blanked. "No, he didn't write anything since The Beatles." But once you start to look, I mean, commercially there are definitely things that outsold anything The Beatles did, like 'Mull of Kintyre'. But critically people don't consider that. **Paul, July 1989**

Linda and Paul, adopting Beatle guise to promote 'Coming Up'.

When 'McCartney' came along I had all these rough things and I liked them all and thought, well, they're rough, but they've got a certain kind of thing about them, so we'll leave it and just put it out. It's not an album which was really sweated over, and yet now I find it's a lot of people's favourite. They think it's great to hear kids screaming and the door opening, it's lovely. **Paul, January 1974**

Wings and Singles: We're a bit vague about singles. We don't sit around and consider policy. We just say: "That would make a good single" and put it out. It's haphazard. **Paul, 1974**

Paul with Denny Laine.

The whole idea behind Wings is to get a touring band. So that we are just like a band, instead of the whole Beatles myth. **Paul, 1976**

There is this feeling that I should mind if they come to see me as a Beatle. But I really don't mind. They're coming to see me; I don't knock it. **Paul, 1976**

On Killing Wings: What do you do, stay stable with a bad group? That's the alternative. I just wasn't happy with the people, so you try and do better. In fact, I've only had about three line-ups of Wings, it's not that many. **Paul, July 1989**

Wings, left to right: Danny Seiwell, Denny Laine, Henry McCullough, Linda and Paul.

I've been told that I was so overbearing. If the guitarists in Wings wanted to play a solo a certain way, I wouldn't dare tell them that it wasn't good. **Paul, October 1986**

The thing about Wings, the difficulty was, being the band after The Beatles. What do you do after The Beatles? I think that any band felt a little bit not up to it. So if you ever had any sort of argument it was amplified. Because they were all insecure. So there were quite a few line-up changes and stuff…If anything, looking from now, the perspective now, it's lucky we ever held a group together. **Paul, 1990**

Paul and Punk in '77: There was a bit of a divide around that time. Strangely enough the only record I had out was 'Mull of Kintyre'. So it certainly was not a question of competing on their level. It was a question of, OK there's a divide so, big deal. And we just released 'Mull of Kintyre'. But I must say at the time I thought, we are kidding, of course, aren't we? Releasing a Scottish waltz in the face of all this furious spitting and gobbing. **Paul, 1990**

Pop v. Pap: Someone's always gonna bitch. There's always gonna be a bad side to everything you do. When I did 'Ebony and Ivory' with Stevie Wonder – which was a perfectly harmless attempt at promoting racial harmony – some people said "Oh, it's just pap." Well – sez you, you know? I mean tough. The point is, there is some kind of black-and-white problem...You can't deny that. I just wanted to do something good, to do a song that I thought might take a little tension out of the situation. **Paul, January 1986**

I'd shied away from Beatles stuff with Wings – it was a bit near to the break-up of The Beatles and it was a painful break-up – a bit like, I hear, a divorce. And the idea was that you don't want to sing any of the ex-wife's songs. And all of us had that feeling independently, wanted to establish a new life after The Beatles. Now, I thought, I don't have to do that any more, I don't have to deny The Beatles songs...So that was a great unblocking.
Paul, December 1990

Paul, Linda and Denny Laine with numerous awards for 'Band On The Run'.

I definitely did miss a collaborator, because even if you've written a thing on your own, it's handy to just take it along to someone. They only have to tell you it's great, that's all the collaboration you need sometimes. Whereas otherwise you're just still wondering if it's good. It's always good to have that little check, second opinion. But I did definitely miss it, obviously, and then I just started. At first I thought, "Well I've collaborated with Lennon and anybody else will not be as good," which I still do feel; if you've written with the best, who else is going to be as good? **Paul, 1990**

'Broad Street': I just got intoxicated with the idea that I'd written it. I started telling people how to write. Should have waited 'til it was a success! We went with it, tried to get committed and go with it as you sometimes do with a bad idea, and it just wasn't very good...I do get letters from fans saying, I love *'Broad Street'* – but they've generally got very thick glasses! **Paul, 1990**

OPPOSITE: Paul, with Lifetime Achievement Award at the 32nd Grammy Awards, Los Angeles, 1990.

On Collaboration: Elvis Costello is a very good foil for me. We foil each other fine. With Elvis it's, you're opinionated, narrow-minded and full of yourself – but I like that in a guy! **Paul, July 1989**

I've found that in writing music over the years that it's often really cool to cut your chords in half and make do with one chord, leave all your melody the same but really space out what's behind it. **Paul, July 1989**

Success and 'Flowers in the Dirt': There was a lot of approval for it – it's a strange album actually – I haven't heard anyone say it was a bad album, though I'm sure there are some. The general consensus seemed to be that it was good...

If I hadn't so much to live up to I would have said it did brilliant – three-and-a-half million or something. For most people that's a pretty big seller, but for Michael Jackson it isn't. If he doesn't do 23 million it's a stiff. **Paul, July 1989**

The current band feels like a very stable band, just in their personalities. There's no piss-artists. We all like a drink, but there's no real serious piss-artist. There's no heavy anything really. Which bands used to be more. They're not like that so much now, which I'm a bit more comfortable with actually. **Paul, 1990**

'All Things Must Pass': I was really a bit paranoid. There was a lot of negativism going down. I felt that whatever happened to my solo album, whether it was a flop or a success, I was going out on my own just to have a bit of peace of mind. For me to do my own album after that – it was joyous. Dream of dreams. Even before I started the album I knew I was going to make a good album because I had so many songs, so much energy. **George, 1975**

Making 'George Harrison': It's the first time I've done a birth, a marriage and a death during making a record. We had a lot of stoppages, but I don't think it really took any longer than any other album to record. **George, 1979**

I hadn't written anything for a year, since 'Thirty-Three & 1/3'. Fuck, what happens if I can't write any more? So one day it's pissing with rain, just coming down in buckets, and I wrote this song. Actually I was a bit embarrassed because it was so simple...but in the end everyone said, "Wow, that's a good one," because people tend to like things simple. Anyway, it turned into 'Blow Away'. **George, 1979**

I racked my brains for weeks and months to try and think of a title because I was trying not to have a song title. In the end I just had to have a title; otherwise the album would never come out, so as it was clouds on the cover, we called it 'Cloud Nine'. **George, 1988**

Harrison on 'Cloud Nine': People think in terms of a comeback, but I really haven't been anywhere. I've been here the whole time. And this record is very much the music I wanted to make. I don't think it's right to try to mould what

George shows off his
British Academy Award.

you do to the current market. It's like the old song says, "Take me as I am or
let me go." This is me; I hope I fit in, but I'm not going to lose any sleep over
it. **George, 1988**

'**Got My Mind Set On You**': The tune's been stuck in my head for twenty
years, although this version is quite different from the original. It rocks along
quite nicely. **George, 1988**

'**When we was Fab**': Well, basically I just thought it would be nice to write a
song with the sound of the '67 or '68 period. It was just a whim, really.
Especially since at that time I was with Jeff Lynne in Australia and I know

how much he likes the old stuff, so I started to write it. I didn't have any lyrics at the time, so it was tentatively called "Aussie Fab" because it was reminiscent of the Fabs and written in Australia. So it was purely a trip down memory lane. **George, 1988**

Ringo's 'Born to Boogie' and 'Son of Dracula' Films: I love directing because you just shout, "Get me this, get me that, move that over there!" It's total control. But I never want to produce again. It's such a headache. Everyone shouts at you! Even though the producer has the authority to shit on everyone else, he's also there to be shat upon, especially if he's as naïve as I was.

I didn't know that if you didn't get the crew home and in their beds by midnight you couldn't work them the next day. 'Cause you see, I'm a musician, and if we start working, and it starts to cook, we'll keep rolling for three days if necessary. But with this movie, it was my first time, it was my stupidity, and I don't blame anyone else. That's what life's about. You have to learn the tricks. **Ringo, 1981**

Ringo in *Caveman*.

Caveman is my first leading role. I haven't been in a movie for years 'cause I'd had enough of just coming on a set for two or three days, doing vignettes like the ones in *Lisztomania* and *Sextette*. So I really enjoyed the chance to go from a weird weakling to the king of the castle in *Caveman*. I'm the hero, you know. And believe it or not it's a family movie. There may be one or two scenes where we get a bit rough, especially when I'm trying to rape Barbara, but it's done in a comic way...It's very slapstick, and there's only fifteen words in the vocabulary. So there's a lot of miming and grunting. They'll be able to understand it even in China! **Ringo, 1981**

I used to get offered film parts just because I was an ex-Beatle. But that doesn't happen any more and now, with *Caveman*, I'll either make it on my own terms or I will end up with egg all over my face. **Ringo, 1980**

I've asked all my friends to help on 'Can't Fight Lightning'. George did a couple of tracks, Paul's done a couple of tracks. But the real drag is that there were tracks made for me by John. I won't use them now, though. Well, I might. You never can tell. But they won't be on this album. The fun was going to be that we'd play together, you know? And we could play real well together – even in 1981. **Ringo, 1981**

John and Yoko Filming *Rape*: We are showing how all of us are exposed and under pressure in our contemporary world. This isn't just about The Beatles. What is happening to the girl on the screen is happening in Biafra, Vietnam, everywhere. **John, 1970**

Recording 'Instant Karma': It was great, you know, because I wrote it in the morning on the piano, and I went to the office and I sang it many times and I sang it, and I said, hell let's do it and we booked the studio, and Phil (Spector) came in and he said "How do you want it?" and I said, you know,

"1950s" and he said "Right," and boom, I did it, in about three goes.
John, 1970

John Lennon/Plastic Ono Band: I didn't really enjoy writing third person songs about people who lived in concrete flats and things like that. I like first person music. But because of my hang-ups, and many other things, I would only now and then specifically write about me. Now I wrote all about me and that's why I like it. It's me! And nobody else. So I like it...It's about me and I don't know about anything else, really. **John, 1970**

Selling singles and being an artist: I'm not going to get hits just like that, people aren't going to buy my album just because *Rolling Stone* liked it...'Mother' is a single. 'Love' is a single. 'God' could be, so could 'Isolation' and 'Remember' I write singles, I write them all the same way. But 'Mother', you've got to take into account the lyrics, too. If I can capture more sales by singing about love than singing about my mother, I'll do it.

I'm opening a door for John Lennon, not for music, or for The Beatles or for a movement or for anything. I'm presenting myself to as broad a scope as I can.

There's that side of the market. I'm not going to disregard it, you know, I mean to sell as many albums as I can, because I'm an artist who wants everybody to love me and everybody to buy my stuff, you know, and I'll go for that. **John, 1970**

John in *How I Won The War.*

It was like our sharing our wedding with whoever wanted to share it with us. We didn't expect a hit record out of it. It was more of a...that's why we called it 'Wedding Album'. You know, people make a wedding album, show it to their relatives when they come around. Well, our relatives are the...what you call fans, or people that follow us outside. So that was our way of letting them join in on the wedding. **John, December 6, 1980**

Recording 'Give Peace a Chance': I sort of cheated. The word Masturbation was in it but I wrote in the lyric sheet, because I'd had enough of the bannings of all...every bloody record I put out was banned for some reason or another. Even 'Walrus' was banned on the BBC at one time, because it said "Knickers." So I mean I'd been banned so many times all over, that I copped out and wrote "Mastication." It was more important to get (the song) out than be bothered by a word, "Masturbation." **John, December 6, 1980**

John, backstage at London's Lyceum, 1969.

Well anyway I took the title and wrote the song 'Woman Is The Nigger Of The World' which I believe was long before Helen Reddy's 'I Am Woman'. So it was the first Women's Liberation song as well, as far as I'm concerned, and it was directly quoted from (Yoko Ono) but (with) her singing it probably would have not got on the air. **John, December 6, 1980**

'Imagine': Well actually that should be credited as a Lennon/Ono song, a lot of it – the lyric and the concept – came from Yoko, but those days I was a bit more selfish, a bit more macho and I sort of omitted to mention her contribution, but it was right out of '*Grapefruit*', her book, there's a whole pile of pieces about imagine this and imagine that and I have given her credit now long overdue. **John, December 6, 1980**

Let's say this last year (1974-5) has been an extraordinary year for me personally. And I'm most amazed that I could get anything out. But I enjoyed doing 'Walls And Bridges' and it wasn't hard when I had the whole thing to go into the studio and do it. I'm surprised it wasn't just all bluuuuggggghhhh. I had the most peculiar year. And I'm just glad that something came out. It describes the year, in a way, but it's not as sort of schizophrenic as the year really was. I think I got such a shock during that year that the impact hasn't come through. It isn't all on 'Walls and Bridges' though. There's a hint of it there. It has to do with age and God knows what else. But only the surface has been touched on 'Walls and Bridges', you know? **John, July 1975**

The last album I did before 'Double Fantasy' was 'Rock n' Roll', with a cover picture of me in Hamburg in a leather jacket. At the end of making that record, I was finishing up a track that Phil Spector had made me sing called 'Just Because' which I really didn't know – all the rest I'd done as a teenager, so I knew them backward – and I just couldn't get the hang of it. At the end of that record – I was mixing it just next door to this very studio – I started spieling and saying, "And so we say farewell from the Record Plant" and a little thing in the back of my mind said, "Are you really saying farewell?" I hadn't thought of it then. I was still separated from Yoko and still hadn't had the baby, but somewhere in the back was a voice that was saying, "Are you saying farewell to the whole game?"

It just flashed by like that – like a premonition. I didn't think of it until a few years later , when I realised that I had actually stopped recording. I came across the cover photo – the original picture of me in my leather jacket, leaning against the wall in Hamburg in 1962 – and I thought, "Is this it? Do I stop where I came in with 'Be-Bop-A-Lula'?" The day I met Paul I was singing that song for the first time onstage. There's a photo in all The Beatles books – a picture of me with a checked shirt on, holding a little acoustic guitar – and I am singing 'Be-Bop-A-Lula', just as I did on that album, and there's the picture of Hamburg and I'm saying goodbye from the Record Plant. **John, December 5, 1980**

Sometimes you wonder, I mean really wonder. I know we make our own reality and we always have a choice, but how much is pre-ordained? Is there always a fork in the road and are there two pre-ordained paths that are equally pre-ordained? There could be hundreds of paths where one could go this way or that way – there's a choice and it's very strange sometimes. **John, December 5, 1980**

Then suddenly it all came to me, all the songs that are on 'Double Fantasy' all came in a period of three weeks in Bermuda after five years of nothing. Not trying but nothing coming anyway, no inspiration, no thought, no anything, then suddenly voom voom voom. **John, December 6, 1980**

All through the taping of 'Starting Over' I was calling what I was doing
"Elvis Orbison": "I want you I need only the lonely." I'm a born-again
rocker, I feel that refreshed, and I'm going right back to my roots...so I go
back to the records I know – Elvis and Roy Orbison and Gene Vincent and
Jerry Lee Lewis. I occasionally get tripped off into 'Walruses' or 'Revolution 9',
but my far-out side has been completely encompassed by Yoko.
John, December 5, 1980

'Woman' came about because, one sunny afternoon in Bermuda, it suddenly
hit me. I saw what women do for us. Not just what my Yoko does for me,
although I was thinking in those personal terms. Any truth is universal. If we'd
made our album in the third person and called it 'Fred and Ada' or 'Tommy'
and had dressed up in clown suits with lipstick and created characters other
than us, maybe a Ziggy Stardust, would it be more acceptable? It's not our
style of art; our life is our art. **John, December 5, 1980**

And if you remember, at the beginning of 'Mother', the first...the beginning of
the album has this bell going dong...dong...dong...It's a church bell which I
slowed down to thirty-three, so it's really like a horror movie, and that was
like the death knell of the Mother-Father-Freudian trip. And if you listen to
the beginning of 'Double Fantasy', you hear ping...ping...ping...Which is
actually a bell that Yoko calls her Wishing Bell. You know, she rings the bell
and makes a wish or whatever...and I put it on 'Double Fantasy', to show the
likeness and the difference of the long, long trip from 'Mother' to 'Starting
Over'. **John, December 6, 1980**

"You're such a lovely audience..."

Live Work

My idea of heaven is not going on the road. John, 1976

It's hard to follow my own act. But the only answer to that would be to give up after The Beatles. I had only two alternatives. Give up or carry on. And having elected to carry on, I couldn't stop. **Paul, February 1990**

My philosophy of a band is, if you can play your stuff in a pub, then you're a good band. **Paul, December 1990**

Put me in front of an audience and I'm afraid I won't ignore them – I can't do the sort of thing Pink Floyd might do. **Paul, December 1990**

Playing Live for the First Time After The Beatles: I wanted some way I could feel easy about appearing live again. It was pretty difficult after The Beatles you know. They weren't interested in playing live except on really big gigs and I was more interested in playing small places and getting near audiences again. A bit like pub rock. **Paul, 1984**

(I was) very nervous. The main thing I didn't want to face was the torment of five rows of press people with little pads all looking and saying "Oh well, he's not as good as he was." So we decided to go on that university tour which made me less nervous because it was less of a big deal. **Paul, January 1974**

Wings Playing it Small in '73: We went off on our little university tour, which was great. It was very ballsy to do, really, but I couldn't think of anything else to do at the time, it just felt like, well what else do I do? Get together a very big famous group with some others?...It's kind of what Ringo and George do. It just felt too safe for me. I just felt, like no – got to risk it a bit more...

Henry McCullough,
Denny Laine and Paul
with Wings, 1974.

We took off on the road. We literally took off in a van up the M1...We kept going until we got to Nottingham University, and then it suddenly hit. Ah, that's it, let's do universities...that's a captive audience...

We just showed up at all these places and it was fairly crazy. We didn't even book hotel rooms. We showed up at 7 o'clock in the evening, and the first thing we'd have to go and do is find a hotel somewhere. There were some shitty places. Talk about a come-down after The Beatles. Really, in a Tranny, a little van with all of us in. Kids, now we had three I think, and a couple of dogs. It was great looking back on it, it was just, phew, did we really do that? **Paul, 1990**

Everything Must be Perfect: It's one of the biggest factors in life. I've come home from some rehearsals with Wings and just got the terrible feeling "It's not right, God we could do much more. We've got to get a producer." But I just have to say to myself: "Get a grip on yourself son. Don't think THAT. You're doing okay." **Paul, 1984**

In the old days of The Beatles we might rehearse for three days. But we've spent months rehearsing Wings. And it's all been better than I thought it would be. **Paul, 1984**

There was one point where we felt (Wings) had to be on stage every night. If we were going to be any good. **Paul, 1984**

Wings and Television Specials: The funny thing was that only the hip people didn't like it. It wasn't a hip show at all. So it wasn't a good show. What do you want from a real, live person? God? But we got millions of letters from mid-America saying they loved the show, I've got to remind myself that the main thing is to enjoy yourself... There's many a person has committed suicide over the fact that his Special wasn't so good. But I wouldn't give a crap. **Paul, 1984**

Wings Playing Banned Songs: The great laugh is when we go live, it makes a great announcement. You can say "This one was banned!" and everyone goes "Hooray!" The audience loves it...Everyone is a bit anti-all-that-banning, all that censorship. Our crew, our generation, really doesn't dig that stuff. **Paul, January 1974**

Playing Live after Wings: I just couldn't be bothered. Until Live Aid came along, I didn't think of doing anything live. Maybe because nobody asked me. Nobody asked me personally, anyway. **Paul, February 1990**

Paul closes the Live Aid concert at London's Wembley Stadium, 1985.

Live-Aid Improvisation: What I like about (performing) is the speed with which your brain reacts. The weirdest one was during the Live-Aid concert when I was singing 'Let It Be', and the mike wasn't on, but I didn't know...And as I'm going through the song I suddenly hear feedback. And it occurred to me to sing, "There will be some feedback, Let It Be." And another part of my brain said, no, don't, this is a serious event, that will be perceived as frivolous. And yet another part of my brain said – feedback, Ethiopia, marvellous, a conceptual link. And in the split second I decided and didn't do it. Thank God. It gives me hot flushes to think about it. **Paul, December 1990**

On Touring 1990: Certain things in rehearsal weren't as fun as they were on records, it wasn't fun to play them – and that was a pretty big criterion. If it's not fun to play I'm not taking it on tour. **Paul, December 1990**

Before you go out, you dread hard questions from the interviewers, you dread the weather in the stadiums, the audiences not liking you, you dread all the dread things. At the end you're like an athlete, you've totally remembered how to do it. For me it was just like being a Beatle, everything was the same. **Paul, 1989**

Imagine looking at Michael Jackson from my perspective. I'm an older rocker, and there's Michael, the hottest thing since sliced-toast. If you're gonna tour you've gotta look at how they do it, and once you look, you see the flaws – you see how ordinary it is, how workaday. **Paul, 1989**

Auto-Pilot: I could be singing 'Yesterday' and wondering what we were going to have for dinner. It's like driving – that thing when you almost fall asleep at the wheel for a second. That can happen when you're performing. **Paul, December 1990**

Keeping it small: We thought are we going to have an army of backing singers? Or an army of people on gongs? But we kept it to six of us and one of the things I was proud of is, at the end of each night, there were only six people holding up their hands. **Paul, December 1990**

I like the working towns. Pittsburgh, Glasgow, Liverpool, Newcastle. I like those people. I'm always more comfortable with that type of a crowd because I feel like I know them. If it's very rich New York Yuppies, I'm not so sure I know 'em or what they're thinking. **Paul, 1989**

Arena Concert Intimacy: What I find now is I get really touched by the audience...Nobody in the audience really sees it. But we do because we're looking at them. And that's the real show. **Paul, February 1990**

You see about the first 20 rows, and these little things flash by, these cameos. We'd often see couples necking – during 'Let It Be', for some reason, people would neck. Which was great because suddenly you could be a voyeur. **Paul, December 1990**

Paul on the road, 1990.

Another night, in Europe somewhere, I've got an image of an older guy – he looked like Neptune, with a great curly beard – and he was crying. It totally touched a nerve. 'Hey Jude'. I was choked, don't look at this guy, look at someone who's laughing, get trivial! Sometimes it goes right through you. He's there with his lovely daughter, and you know that he's brought her along to say, "This is what I was doing in the '60s." **Paul, 1989**

On Playing Beatles Songs: People would have signs saying, "I've waited 20 years for this." That was what was great about doing 'Pepper', 'Jude', those old songs.

What's nice about 'Sgt Pepper' is the way John and I conceived it, it's all directed to an audience: "Splendid time guaranteed for all"...The whole idea of 'Pepper' is a show, a circus. This song works great live 'cause you're saying, "You're such a lovely audience we'd love to take you home with us."...And then 'Hey Jude' I realised I'd never done. God I thought this is great "nah na na na-na-na-nah" – I've got an audience participation number, which I always wanted. I love them. **Paul, December 1990**

Playing John's Songs: Someone suggested, "Why don't you do one of John's (songs), that'd be really poignant." And it would, I don't know, you've got to deal with the emotion of something like that. But it'd be nice to make a nod, or a wink, to the lad. He was a great, a major influence in my life, as I suppose I was on his. **Paul, July 1989**

In fact, I considered doing a major tribute to John. But it suddenly felt too precious, too showbiz. I was going to have a whacking great picture of John and just say, "He was my friend." Which was true. I'm totally proud to have worked with him.

But then people started saying, "Why don't you do 'Imagine'?" And I thought, Fucking hell, Diana Ross does 'Imagine'. They all do 'Imagine'. That's when I backed off the whole thing. You go on tour, you sing your songs, arrange 'em nice, do it, and if you do it well enough, that's what people will remember. **Paul, August 1990**

I was going to do one of my songs called 'Here Today' (from the 1982 'Tug of War' album), it's about John. It's a song saying, "If you were here today you'd probably say what I'm doing is a load of crap, but you wouldn't mean it, 'cos you're like me really. I know." It's one of those "Come out from behind yer glasses, John and look at me" kind of things. And it was a kind of love song really, not to John, but about John and my relationship with him. **Paul, July 1989**

Remembering John in Liverpool: I thought it would be nice to just do a little something. I didn't want to go crazy with it. I didn't want any "Oh sacred memory of the great loved one." I didn't want to get too precious with it. But I did feel good about just popping a little medley together like that: they're nice songs to sing, and given the emotion of me singing John's songs, for the first time in my life, it had to be Liverpool. So I finally got to sing John's part on 'Help!' and 'Strawberry Fields' which was always one of my favourite John tracks. **Paul, 1989**

Still Rockin' at Fifty?: Everyone was asking, "Is this your last tour, Paul?" And I'd say, "Look, it's just because we're at this great 'venereal age' as my dad used to say, this venerable age." They naturally think it's my last tour...But as the tour went on I was thinking, Jesus, I'm feeling better and better each day. Your stamina improves, you've got to do two hours' work-out each night, so you don't have to jog. You're physically working. So I think we'll probably go out towards the end of next year. It feels good. After all this it still feels good. **Paul, 1989**

George Organises the Bangladesh Relief Concert: Up until the time we decided to do the concert, there had been very little that I had actually read about (Bangladesh). I'd heard a little bit on television in England...It's a particularly bad situation...But it happens all the time...

I was asked by a friend to help, that's all. This was Ravi Shankar's idea. He wanted to do something about it...Once I decided I was going to go on the show, then I organized the thing with a little help from my friends. Some of the musicians flew thousands of miles and didn't get paid for anything. They were really into the whole idea of helping the refugees. **George, 1988**

George and Charity: When I did Bangladesh, I spent a couple of months, every day and night, on the telephone, trying to trick people into doing it and making a commitment. Nowadays, you phone somebody up, and it's an accepted part of life that every so often you give something to charity. **George, February 1987**

George on the road, 1974.

Getting Dylan to Play Bangladesh: He never committed himself right up until the moment he came onstage...

   He turned up (the morning of the concert) which looked positive, and we travelled down to Madison Square Garden (in New York). So I had a list, sort of a running order that I had glued on my guitar. When I got to the point Bob was going to come on, I had "Bob" with a question mark. I looked over my shoulder to see if he was around, because if he wasn't, I would have to go on to the next bit. And I looked around and he was so nervous – he had his guitar on and his shades – he was sort of coming on, coming. He was just coming! So I just said, "My old friend Bob Dylan!" It was only at that moment that I knew for sure he was going to do it. Then we did the second show. And after the second show he picked me up and hugged me and he said, "God! If only we'd done three shows!" **George, November 1987**

Paul and the Bangladesh Benefit Concert: George came up and asked me if I wanted to play Bangladesh and I thought, blimey, what's the point? We've just broken up and we're joining up again? It just seemed a bit crazy. **Paul, January 1974**

Bangladesh was caca. **John, September 1980**

George on Tour in 1974: I know we get ten people who say the show sucks every night. And we get a hundred who, when we ask them did they like the show, say: "We got much more than we ever hoped for."

   I don't care if nobody comes to see me, nobody ever buys another record of me. I don't give a shit, it doesn't matter to me, but I'm going to do what I feel within myself. **George, 1974**

Audience Interaction: I don't know how it feels down there, but from up here you seem pretty dead. **George, 1974**

On Ending Touring: There was one thing that sticks in my mind. On one of the concerts, I think it was Long Beach (California), instead of leaving right after the show, I waited until all the audience had gone. I was just hanging around the stadium, and I watched them bulldozing. They had a bulldozer in the middle...and they were bulldozing all the rubble left by the audience. There were mountains of empty bottles of gin and bourbon and tequila and brassieres and shoes and coats and trash. I mean it was unbelievable.

Another thing – you know, that rock band I was in, they were some pretty heavy-duty people. We had been known in the past to smoke some reefer ourselves...there was so much reefer going about. And I don't know, I just thought, "Do I actually have anything in common with these people?"

Even now, after the Prince's Trust (Prince Charles' personal charitable organisation) people said "Oh doesn't it make you want to go on the road?" I said "No. It doesn't." It doesn't because it's tiring, and just being stuck in some crummy motel in Philadelphia is not my idea of having fun. I mean I wouldn't mind doing shows here and there, but it's tiring. It is very tiring. **George, November 1987**

Fans and Security: I'm not really worried about being in public. I'm not crazy about being in crowds, though...I prefer peace and quiet. But I don't really worry about anything like that. The only time is if you get a mob of people who know you're going to be somewhere. I mean, there's always fanatics at rock concerts. But to do a tour wouldn't be any trouble because you have all the security and you know the way in and the way out and it's no bother, really.

I don't fear for my life like some people try to suggest. They've said, since John Lennon got killed, I would go and hide and I've had a big fence built around my property. I had a fence around my property back in 1965, so there's no change really. **George, 1988**

Ringo Starr and His All-Starr Band: Last year I was sittin' 'round wondering what I was gonna do now that I don't drink and take stuff any more...then suddenly, like a bolt out of the blue, I heard this voice saying to meself, "Well, you are a drummer. And it's the most boring thing in the world to be a drummer if you don't have any people in front of you. There's very little melody in front of the drums." So I just pulled out me old phone books, and looked up a few names. Everyone of them, every single one was in me phone books. **Ringo, 1989**

On the Road for the First Time Since 1966: After Joe (Walsh) said yes, I told him we'd been offered 30 gigs and in my naïvety I said, "Well, we can do six a week you know, and get it over with." Anyway, Joe asked me how long it was since I'd been on tour and explained that three shows a week is great, four is OK and five is stretching it. **Ringo, 1989**

Ringo drums with the Beach Boys at their 4th of July concert in Washington, 1983.

The others had to be very patient with me because I had to learn all my songs again. I'd sung a tune like 'Yellow Submarine' on the record but I'd never played it live. I'd actually stopped. I mean, I'd turned up to a lot of gigs over the years and I was always getting up to play. But though I've got photographs of me playing all over the world, I've absolutely no memory of any of it. And I've never practised on my own in a back room. The great discovery this time was that I could still play at all. **Ringo, 1989**

The worst band I ever played with in my life had Eric Clapton, Elton John, Keith Richards, Ronnie Wood and I all playing in my studio in Tittenhurst in 1985. Too many leaders. It just didn't work. Whereas with this band (Ringo's All-Starr Band) there was a really magical atmosphere, and a feeling that everybody was out there to do it for each other. Everyone admired everyone else. **Ringo, 1989**

Ringo on Drums: The love of my life, the dream I'd had when I was 13 and which, in a haze of alcohol, I'd gradually forgotten.

The support in America for acts who are getting their act together again is so brilliant. When we did the 'No No Song' and I sang "No, no, I don't take it no more," they all understood it. **Ringo, 1989**

For the first week it felt real strange to be playing, 'cos I'm an old rocker and after the show you go crazy, right? So after these shows one half of me brain was goin', "Let's go crazy!" and the other half was goin' "We don't do that now!" **Ringo, 1989**

John un-Beatled: The first show we (John & Yoko) did together was at Cambridge University in 1968 or '69 when she had been booked to do a concert with some jazz musicians. That was the first time I had appeared un-Beatled. I just hung around and played feedback, and people got very upset because they recognised me: "What's he doing here?" It's always: "Stay in your bag." So when she tried to rock, they said, "What's she doing here?" And when I went with her and tried to be the instrument and not project...well, even some of the jazz guys got upset. **John, December 5, 1980**

The point of the Bed-In in a nutshell was a commercial for Peace, as opposed to a commercial for War, which was on the news every day those days in the newspapers...What the Bed-In was seven days – because the press were always asking questions, asking questions. Seven days that they can ask anything – no secrets, no time limit...till you've got everything you need to know about John and Yoko. **John, December 6, 1980**

The press came in expecting to see us fucking in bed – they all heard John and Yoko were going to fuck in front of the press for peace...We were a married couple in bed talking about Peace. It was one of our greater episodes. **John, 1970**

The best thing we did in a bag together was a press conference in Vienna...It was like a hotel press conference. We kept them out of the room. We came down the elevator in the bag and we went in and we got comfortable and they were all ushered in. It was a very strange scene because they'd never seen us before...A few people were saying "C'mon get out of the bags." And we wouldn't let them see us. They all stood back saying "Is it really John and Yoko?" and "What are you wearing and why are you doing this?" We said, "This is total communication with no prejudice." It was just great. **John, 1970**

'Yer Blues' Live: It was instantly creative, and there was no big palaver. It wasn't like this set format show that I'd been doing with The Beatles, where you'd go on and do these numbers 'I Wanna Hold Your Head' [sic], you know. And the show lasts twenty minutes and nobody's listening, they're just screaming, and the amps are as big as a peanut. It was more of a spectacular rather than rock 'n' roll.

OPPOSITE: **John on stage
with the Plastic Ono
Band at the UNICEF
Benefit concert at
London's Lyceum, 1969.**

Whereas actually the first time I performed without The Beatles for years
was the Rock and Roll Circus, and it was great to be on stage with Eric
(Clapton) and Keith Richard and a different noise coming out behind me,
even though I was still singing and playing the same style. It was just a great
experience. I thought, wow, it's fun with other people.
John, December 6, 1980

'Some Time In New York City' Live: That was a heavy show, and a lot of the
audience walked out, you know. But the ones that stayed, they were in a
trance, man. They just all came to the front, because it was one of the first
real Heavy Rock shows, where we had a good, good band and that John and
Yoko did together. And I always think that some of those kids...formed those
freaky bands later, because there were about two hundred kids at the front
there, somewhere about thirteen, fourteen, fifteen, who were looking at Yoko
and looking at us the way we were playing that 'Don't Worry, Kyoko', and it
really reached a peak of whatever you call it.

It really went out there that night. And I often think – I wonder if...you
know, I hear touches of our early stuff in a lot of the Punk New Wave stuff. I
could hear licks and flips coming out. And I...it pleases me, it pleases both of
us. I think...I bet...I'd love to know, were they in the audience? And did
somebody go and form a group in London because it sounds...sure as hell
sounds like it. **John, December 6, 1980**

U.S. Government Harassment and Hurting John's Work: It did. It did.
There's no denying it. In '72 it was really getting to me. Not only was I
physically having to appear in court cases, it just seemed like a toothache that
wouldn't go away...There was a period when I was hangin' out with a group
called Elephant's Memory. And I was ready to go on the road for pure fun. I
didn't want to go on the road for money. That was the time when I was
standing up in the Apollo with a guitar at the Attica relatives' benefit or

ending up on the stage at the John Sinclair rally. I felt like going on the road and playing music. And whatever excuse – charity or whatever – would have done me. But they kept pullin' me back in court! I had the group hangin' 'round, but finally I had to say, "Hey, you better get on with your lives." Now, the last thing on earth I want to do is perform. That's a direct result of the immigration thing. In '71, 1972, I wanted to go out and rock my balls off onstage and I just stopped. **John, June 1975**

John Lennon's Last Live Appearance: Through a mutual friend (Elton John) asked if 'Whatever Gets You Through the Night' got to be number one, would I appear on stage with him, and I said "Sure" not thinking in a million years it was going to get to number one...And there I was, on stage.

I was moved by it, but everybody else was in tears. I felt guilty 'cause I wasn't in tears. I just went up and did a few numbers. But the emotional thing was me and Elton together (playing 'Lucy in the Sky with Diamonds')...He has this sort of Beatle thing from way back....well, it meant a lot to me and it meant a hell of a lot to Elton, and he was in tears. It was a great high night, a really high night and...Yoko and I met backstage. And somebody said, "Well, there's two people in love." That was before we got back together...It was very weird.

She came backstage and I didn't know she was there, 'cause if I'd known she was there I'd've been too nervous to go on, you know, I would have been terrified. She was backstage afterwards, and there was just that moment when we saw each other and like, it's like in the movies, you know, when time stands still? And there was silence, everything went silent, y'know, and we were just sort of lookin' at each other and...oh, hello. I knew she'd sent Elton and I a flower each, and we were wearing them onstage, but I didn't know she was there and then everybody was around us and flash flash flash. But there was that moment of silence. And somebody observed it and told me later on, after we were back together again, and said "A friend of mine saw you backstage and thought if ever there was two in love, it's those two." And I thought, well, it's weird somebody noticed it...So it was a great night... **John, June 1975**

John's last concert appearance with Elton John at Madison Square Garden, New York, 1974.

"Get back to where you once belonged..."

Rock & Roll

The Beatles at Abbey Road, 1963.

There is nothing conceptually better than rock and roll. No group, be it Beatles, Dylan, or Stones has ever improved on 'A Whole Lotta Shakin'' for my money. Or maybe I'm like our parents, you know, that's my period and I dig it, and I'll never leave it...It will never be as new and it will never do what it did then. John, 1970

Rock is becoming too intellectualised. But the good thing is with every movement in that direction there is a counter movement. Someone, somewhere starts up. Like the pub rock bands. It's a small scene but it's healthy. It starts to counteract the big deal of it all. Our university tour was well received. (Wings) wasn't the greatest band in the world but just the fact we were there went down well. **Paul, 1974**

Paul and John at the Casbah in Liverpool, 1959.

The whole thing with punk rock was boring old farts. That was the expression that came in. Obviously there was the age difference. They were doing what we had done ten years before. So that gave them edge that we'd had when we did it. Youth, there's an edge to youth you can't deny. But there's also an ignorance to youth too...And all they had was youth, really, just the innocence of it all. It was good, it was the new broom. It was all getting a bit Rod Stewart in LA at that time. It was all getting a little bit decadent, I think. So it was all right. **Paul, 1990**

George on Bob Dylan: He's fantastic, you know. There's not a lot of people in the world who I see from a historical point of view. Five hundred years from now, looking back in history, I think he will still be the man, Bob, he just takes the cake. **George, 1987**

Rap music is just computerised crap. I listen to *Top of the Pops* and after three songs I feel like killing someone. **George, 1989**

Sometimes I listen to the English pop scene and wonder was it worth all that, trying to get it...I mean, we always thought – not like a heavy conscious thing – but to try and get it somewhere good. Now there's just so much crap going down. I don't enjoy any of it. **Ringo, January 1974**

The Carl Perkins TV special, left to right: Dave Edmunds, George, Carl Perkins, Eric Clapton, Roseanne Cash, Ringo.

(Rock and roll) is primitive enough and has no bullshit, really, the best stuff, and it gets through to you its beat. Go to the jungle and they have the rhythm and it goes throughout the world and it's as simple as that. You get the rhythm going, everybody gets into it.

I read that Eldridge Cleaver said that blacks gave the middle-class whites back their bodies, you know, put their minds and bodies together through the music. It is something like that, it gets through, to me it got through, it was the only thing to get through to me after all the things that were happening when I was 15. Rock and roll was real, everything else was unreal. And the thing about rock and roll, good rock and roll, whatever good means, is that it's real, and realism gets through to you despite yourself. You recognize something in it which is true, like all true art. Whatever art is, readers, okay? If it's real, it's simple usually, and if it's simple, it's true, something like that. Rock and roll got through to you, finally. **John, 1970**

The Blues: It's real, it's not perverted or thought about, it's not a concept, it is a chair, not a design for a chair, or a better chair, or a bigger chair, or a chair with leather or with design...it is the first chair. It is a chair for sitting on, not chairs for looking at or being appreciated. You sit on that music. **John, 1970**

The Future of Rock and Roll: Whatever we make it. If we want to go bullshitting off into intellectualism with rock and roll, we are going to get bullshitting rock intellectualism. If we want real rock and roll, it's up to all of us to create it and stop being hyped by, you know, revolutionary image and long hair. We've got to get over that bit. That's what cutting hair is all about. Let's own up now and see who's who, who's doing something about what, and who's making music and who's laying down bullshit. Rock and roll will be whatever we make it. **John, 1970**

Yoko's whole thing was that scream. Listen to 'Don't Worry Kyoko'. It's one of the fuckin' best rock and roll records ever made. Listen to it and play 'Tutti Frutti'...You see, I'm digressing from mine, but if somebody with a rock-oriented mind can possibly listen to her stuff you'll see what she is doing. It's fantastic. It's as important as anything (The Beatles) ever did and as important as anything the Stones or Townshend ever did. Listen to it and you'll hear what she's putting down.

On 'Cold Turkey' I'm getting towards it. I'm influenced by her music 1,000 percent more than I ever was by Dylan. She makes music like you've never heard on earth. And when the musicians play with her they're inspired out of their skulls...It's fantastic. It's like 20 years ahead of its time.
John, 1970

The Superstar Rock Club and Generosity: It was around before. It's harder when you're on the make to be generous, 'cause you're all competing. But once you're sort of up there, wherever it is...The rock papers love to write about jet-setting rock stars and they dig it and we dig it in a way. The fact is that, yeah, I see Mick, I see Paul, I see Elton, they're all my contemporaries and I've known the other Beatles, of course, for years, and Mick for ten years, and we've been hangin' around since 'Rock Dreams'. And suddenly it's written up that we're trying to form a club. But we always were a club. We always knew each other. It just so happens that it looks more dramatic in the paper. **John, June 1975**

Take Mick for instance. Mick's put out consistently good work for twenty years and will they give him a break? Will they ever say, "Look at him, he's Number One," he's thirty-six and he's put out a beautiful song, 'Emotional Rescue', it's up there. I enjoyed it, lots of people enjoyed it. So it goes up and down, up and down. God help Bruce Springsteen when they decide he's no

Paul and John fronting
The Quarrymen, 1957.

longer God...All he has to do is look at me and Mick...I cannot be a punk in
Hamburg and Liverpool any more. I'm older now. I see the world through
different eyes. I still believe in love, peace and understanding, as Elvis
Costello said, and what's so funny about love, peace and understanding?
John, December 5, 1980

Rock & Roll Dinosaurs: You know, they're congratulating the Stones on
being together 112 years. Whoooopee! At least Charlie and Bill still got their
families. In the Eighties they'll be asking, "Why are those guys still together?
Can't they hack it on their own? Why do they have to be surrounded by a
gang? Is the little leader scared somebody's gonna knife him in the back?"
That's gonna be the question. That's-a-gonna be the question!

They're gonna look back at The Beatles and the Stones and all those guys
are relics. The days when those bands were just all men will be on the
newsreels, you know. They will be showing pictures of the guy with lipstick
wriggling his ass and the four guys with the evil black make-up on their eyes
trying to look raunchy. That's gonna be the joke in the future, not a couple
singing together or living and working together. It's all right when you're 16,
17, 18 to have male companions and idols, okay? It's tribal and it's gang and
it's fine. But when it continues and you're still doing it when you're 40, that
means you're still 16 in the head. **John, September 1980**

"I get high with a little help from my friends..."

Drugs

I've always needed a drug to survive. The others too, but I always had more. I always took more pills, more of everything because I'm crazy probably. John, 1970

I was the first one on coke in (The Beatles), which horrified the whole group, and I just thought, no sweat. The minute I stopped, the whole record industry has got into it and has never stopped since. **Paul, October 1986**

There's a story that sums up the whole drugs thing. When I went out to LA at the time of that 'Pussy Cats' album I was offered angel dust. What is it? and they said, It's an elephant tranquiliser, and I said to the guy, Is it fun? He thought for a moment and said, No, it's not fun.

So, I said, OK, I won't have any then. That sums it up, you know. You had anything, man, even if it wasn't fun! You sort of had to do it – peer pressure...I remember John going on Old Grey Whistle Test and saying, Paul only took (LSD) four times! We all took it twenty times!! It was as if you'd score points. **Paul, October 1986**

Paul on John's Heroin Addiction: I really didn't like that. Unfortunately, he was driftin' away from us at that point, so none of us actually knew. He never told us; we heard rumours and we were very sad. But he'd embarked on a new course, which really involved anything and everything. Because John was that kind of guy – he wanted to live life to the full as he saw it. He would often say things like, "If you find yourself at the edge of a cliff and you wonder whether you should jump or not – try jumping." **Paul, January 1986**

Linda and me came over for dinner once and John said, "You fancy getting the trepanning thing done?" I said, "Well, what is it?" and he said, "Well, you kind of have a hole bored into your skull and it relieves the pressure."

We're sitting at dinner and this is seriously being offered!

Now this wasn't a joke, this was like, Let's go next week, we know a guy who can do it and maybe we can do it all together. So I said, "Look, you go and have it done, and if it works, great. Tell us about it and we'll all have it."

But I'm afraid I've always been a bit cynical about stuff like that – thank God! – because I think that there's so much crap that you've got to be careful of. But John was more open to things like that. **Paul, October 1986**

Hashish and Paul's Imprisonment in Japan on Drug Charges: I can take it or leave it. It's silly to say it's wicked. I think we should decriminalise it. I wasn't badly treated (in jail) but it was an experience I never want to repeat. It was incredibly dumb, really stupid of me to try to take the hash into Japan. I just wasn't thinking logically. I didn't really try to hide the stuff. It was just sitting on top of the suitcase. **Paul, 1984**

I must say – and at the risk of sounding goody-goody again – that I personally feel, from this perspective, today, that my favourite thing is to be clean and straight. I think you can enjoy your life better that way. I mean, when we were very straight in The Beatles, we did music that was pretty much as far out as the stuff we did later. Maybe it wasn't as far out, but actually, beneath the surface, it was every bit as meaningful.
Paul, January 1986

George Protesting His Drug Possession Conviction: I'm a tidy sort of bloke, I don't like chaos. I kept records in the record rack, tea in the tea caddy, and pot in the pot box. This was the biggest stick of hash I have ever seen and obviously I'd have known about it if I'd seen it before. Those who think this is a low down dirty thing to smoke pot will be further convinced they're right and we're wrong. But it will strengthen the others who follow us. We were once everybody's darlings. But it isn't like that any more. They hate us.
George, 1969

Up until LSD, I never realised that there was anything beyond this state of consciousness. But all the pressure was such that, like the man (Bob Dylan) said, "There must be some way out of here." I think for me it was definitely LSD. The first time I took it, it just blew everything away. I had such an incredible feeling of well-being, that there was a God and I could see Him in every blade of grass. It was like gaining hundreds of years of experience within twelve hours. It changed me and there was no way back to what I was before. It wasn't all good, because it left a lot of questions as well. And we still had to continue being fab, you know? And now with that added perspective. It wasn't easy. **George, November 1987**

I hadn't had any psychedelic drugs for almost ten years since the '60s when we were all loonies, so I thought maybe I should have it to just see...if it reminds me of anything...You have to be careful (with mushrooms) because they're so good. That stuff is very organic, you know. You feel great, and everything is in perfect focus, even the physical body feels good. But because I felt so good, I kept on eating them all day. I nearly did myself in; I had too many. I fell over and left my body, hit my head on a piece of concrete – but they were great. **George, 1979**

(LSD) can help you go from A to B, but when you get to B, you see C. And you see that to get really high, you have to go it straight. So this was the disappointing thing about LSD. In the physical world we live in, there's always duality – good and bad, black and white, yes and no. There's always something equal and opposite to everything, and this is why you can't say LSD is good or it's bad, because it's good and bad. It's both of them and it's neither of them altogether...

The hippies are a good idea – love, flowers, and that is great – but when you see the other half of it, it's like anything. I love all these people, too, those who are honest and trying to find a bit of truth and to straighten out the untruths. I'm with them one-hundred percent, but when I see the bad side of it, I'm not so happy. **George, 1988**

I just got caught up in that strange belief that if you're creative you have to be brain damaged. I went through the whole thing whereby I was so deranged I wasn't creative. I was too busy taking stuff to do anything. If you listen to the records you can hear them all going downhill. I was taking less and less interest in recording and promoting them.

By 1980 I could not write any more and I was just that personality person. I would be at all the parties with me bow tie on. The only crowd I hung out with were all addicted. If you were straight I wouldn't have you in my house. But I wasn't creating anything. Unless you wanna call 'Thomas the Tank Engine and Friends' creating something. And in the end I couldn't even get a record deal. I wasn't hungry any more. I'm still not hungry now, but I do wanna play. **Ringo, January 1991**

The only time Yoko and I took heavy drugs was when we were without hope. And the only way we got out of this was with hope. And if we can sustain the hope, we don't need liquor, hard drugs, or anything. But if we lose hope, what can you do? What is there to do? **John, June 1970**

LSD: It went on for years. I must have had a thousand trips...I used to just eat it all the time. **John, 1970**

Heroin? It was not too much fun. I never injected it or anything. (Yoko and I) sniffed a little when we were in real pain. I mean we just couldn't...people were giving us such a hard time. **John, 1970**

I think George was pretty heavy on (LSD), we are probably both the most cracked. Paul is a bit more stable than George and I...I think LSD profoundly shocked (Paul) and Ringo. I think maybe they regret it. **John, 1970**

John Separated from Yoko for Eighteen Months: I was like a chicken without a head. I'd be waking up in strange places, or reading about myself in the paper, doing extraordinary things, half of which I'd done and half of which I hadn't done. And find myself in a sort of mad dream for a year. You can put it down to which night with which bottle, or which night in which town. **John, June 1975**

John and Harry Nilsson are ejected from the Troubador Club in Los Angeles after John had heckled the Smothers Brothers, 1974.

It was a pretty hectic period, pretty wild and it sounds funny in retrospect but it was pretty miserable, yeah, a pretty bad period – and I'm thankful that I'm out of it and I don't drink now because it scares me, you know even a glass of wine knocks me out now, so I'm happy about that, forget about the booze. **John, December 6, 1980**

"Within you, without you..."

Religion & Philosophy

Henry Ford knew how to sell cars by advertising. I'm selling peace, and Yoko and I are just one big advertising campaign. It may make people laugh, but it may make them think, too. Really, we're Mr. and Mrs. Peace. John, 1969

I don't like religion as such because there's always wars with every bloody religion. **Paul, July 1989**

With life and all the stuff I've been through, I do have a belief in, I don't know what it is, in goodness, in a good spirit. I generally think that what people have done with religion is personified good and evil, so good's become God with an "o" out, and evil's become Devil with a "d" added. That's my theory of religion. **Paul, July 1989**

It is one of our perennial problems, whether there is a God. From the Hindu point of view each soul is divine. All religions are branches of one big tree. It doesn't matter what you call Him as long as you call. **George, 1973**

George with Ravi
Shankar (centre).

Just as cinematic images appear to be real but are only combinations of light and shade, so is the universal variety a seeming delusion. The planetary spheres, with their countless forms of life, are naught but figures in a cosmic motion picture...One's values are profoundly changed when he is finally convinced that creation is only a vast motion picture; and that not in, but beyond it, lies his own reality. **George, 1973**

If there is a God, I want to see him. It's pointless to believe in something without proof, and Krishna consciousness and meditation are methods where you can actually obtain God perception. You can actually see God and hear Him, play with Him. It might sound crazy, but He's actually there with you. **George, 1973**

Through Hinduism, I feel a better person. I just get happier and happier. I now feel for a fact that I am unlimited, and I am more in control of my own physical body. The thing is, you go to an ordinary church and it's a nice feeling. They all tell you about God, but they don't show you the way. They don't show you how to become Christ-conscious yourself. Hinduism is different. **George, 1972**

Gandhi says create and preserve the image of your choice. The image of my choice is not Beatle George. But why live in the past? Be here now, and now, whether you like me or not, is where I am.

Fuck it, my life belongs to me. It actually doesn't. It belongs to him. My life belongs to the Lord Krishna and there's me dog collar to prove it. I'm just a dog and I'm led around by me dog collar by Krishna. I'm just the servant of the servant of the servant of the servant of the servant of Krishna. That's how I feel. Never been so humble in all my life, and I feel great. **George, 1974**

Hippie Philosophy: I don't mind anybody dropping out of anything. But it's the imposition on somebody else I don't like. The moment you start dropping out and then begging off somebody else to help you, then it's no good. It doesn't matter what you are as long as you work. It doesn't matter if you chop wood as long as you chop and keep chopping. Then you get what's coming to you. You don't have to drop out. In fact, if you drop out you put yourself further away from the goal of life than if you were to keep working. **George, 1983**

Life & Humour: Well, I am two-faced. But really, things serious and comical are like night and day, black and white, yin and yang. In order to be comical, you have to be serious. You can't have one without the other. The world is a very serious and, at times, very sad place – but at other times it is all such a joke. **George, 1978**

George and Religion in '88: I keep it to myself unless somebody asks me about it. But I still feel the same as I felt back in the '60s. I lost touch with the Krishnas when Prabhupada (the founder and leader of the Krishna faith) died, maybe ten years ago or something. I knew one or two of them, but I don't really hang out with them any more. I used to go and see the old master, you know, A. C. Bhaktivedanta, quite a lot. He was real good. I'm still involved but it's something which is more like a thing you do inside yourself. You don't actually do it in the road. It's a way of just trying to get in touch with yourself.

I still write songs with it in there in little bits and pieces, but lots of songs that are unfinished say various things but maybe I say it in different ways now. There's a song on this album ('Cloud Nine') which is straight out of Yogananda, 'Fish on the Sand' it's called. **George, 1988**

George and the Irrelevance of Armageddon: In one way I feel pessimistic. When you see the rate that the world is being demolished – people polluting the oceans and chopping down all the forests – unless somebody puts the brakes on soon, there isn't going to be anything left. There's just going to be more and more people with less and less resources. In that respect, I feel very sad. But at the same time, I have to be optimistic.

At the bottom line, I think that even if the whole planet blew up, you'd

have to think about what happens when you die. In the end, "Life goes on within you and without you." I just have a belief that this is only one little bit, the physical world is one little bit, of the physical universe, and you can't really destroy it totally. You can destroy our planet, but the souls are going onto other planets. So in the end it doesn't really matter.
George, November 1987

I won't go to funerals because I don't believe in them. I totally believe your soul has gone by the time you get into the limo. She or he's up there or wherever it is. I'm sure...I can't wait to go half the time. **Ringo, 1980**

Ringo enjoys a game of pool with Keith Moon.

I believe that God is like a power-house, like where you keep electricity, like a power station. And He's the supreme power, and that He's neither good nor bad, left, right, black or white. He just is. And we tap that source of power and make it what we will. Just as electricity can kill people in a chair, or you can light a room with it. I think God is. **John, June 1970**

John's Philosophy: Peace, just no violence, and everybody grooving, if you don't mind the word. Of course, we all have violence in us, but it must be channelled or something. If I have long hair, I don't see why everyone else should have long hair. And if I want peace, I'll suggest peace to everyone. But I won't hustle them up for peace. If people want to be violent, let them not interfere with people who don't want violence. Let them kill each other if there has to be that. You either get tired fighting for peace or you die.
John, June 1970

I was a hitter. I couldn't express myself and I hit. I fought men and I hit women. That is why I am always on about peace, you see. It is the most violent people who go for love and peace...I will have to be a lot older before I can face in public how I treated women as a youngster.
John, September 1980

We're all responsible for war. We all must do something, no matter what – by growing our hair long, standing on one leg, talking to the press, having bed-ins – to change the attitudes. The people must be made aware that it's up to them. Bed-ins are something that everybody can do and they're so simple. (Yoko and I are) willing to be the world's clowns to make people realise it.
John, February 1969

In (Yoko's and my) pleas for peace I refuse to be a leader and I'll always show my genitals or do something which prevents me from being Martin Luther King or Gandhi and getting killed. Because that's what happens to leaders... **John, 1972**

(Yoko and I) are both artists. Peace is our art...We stand a chance of influencing other young people. And it is they who will rule the world tomorrow. **John, 1969**

If anybody thinks our (peace vote) campaign is naïve, that's their opinion and that's okay. Let them do something else and if (Yoko and I) like their ideas, we'll join in with them. But until then, we'll do it the way we are. We're artists, not politicians. Not newspapermen, not anything. We do it in the way that suits us best, and this is the way we work.

John and Yoko in Amsterdam during their peace crusade, 1969.

Publicity and things like that is our game. The Beatles' thing was that. And that was the trade I've learned. This is my trade, and I'm using it to the best of my ability. **John, June 1970**

We must be one country and stick together. You don't have to have badges to say we're together. We're together if we're together, and no stamps or flags are going to make anybody together...folks. **John, June 1970**

Inevitable World Revolution: I've got no more conception than you (on how it will happen), I can't see...eventually it will happen, like it will happen...it has to happen, what else can happen? It might happen now, or it might happen in 50 or 100 years...

I'm back to where I was when I was 17; at 17 I used to think I wish a fuckin' earthquake or revolution would happen so that I could go out and steal and do what the blacks are doing now. If I was black I'd be all for it, if I were 17 I'd be all for it because what have you got to lose? And now I've got nothing to lose. I don't want to die, and I don't want to be hurt physically, but fuck, if they blow the world up, fuck, we're all out of our pain then, forget it! No more problems.

I'm saying "Hold on John" too because I don't want to die. I'm a coward...well, I'm not a coward, but I don't want to die, I don't want to be hurt and please don't hit me. **John, 1970**

Violence and Revolution: I want to see the plan. That is what I used to say to Abbie Hoffman and Jerry Rubin. Count me out if it is for violence. Don't expect me to be on the barricades unless it is with flowers.
John, September 1980

I regret profoundly that I was not an American and not born in Greenwich Village. That's where I should have been. It never works that way. Everybody heads towards the centre, that's why I'm here now. I'm here just to breathe it. It might be dying and there might be a lot of dirt in the air that you breathe, but this is where it's happening. You go to Europe to rest, like in the country. It's so overpowering, America, and I can't take much of it, it's too much for me. **John, 1970**

John & Living in America: I have a love for this country. If it were two thousand years ago, we'd all want to live in Rome. This is Rome now.
John, September 1976

Reality and Music: Language and song is to me, apart from being pure vibrations, just like trying to describe a dream. And because we don't have telepathy or whatever it is, we try and describe the dream to each other, to verify to each other what we know, what we believe is inside each other. And the stuttering is right – because we can't say it. No matter how you say it, it's never how you want to say it.

As soon as you find the pattern, you break it. Otherwise it gets boring. The Beatles' pattern is one that has to be scrapped. If it remains the same, it's

a monument or a museum, and one thing this age is about is no museums. The Beatles turned into a museum, so they have to be scrapped or deformed or changed.

(We are moving towards) complete freedom and non-expectation from audience or musician or performer. And then, when we've had that for a few hundred years, then we can talk about playing around with patterns and bars and music again. We must get away from the patterns we've had for these thousands of years. **John, June 1970**

As soon as you've clutched onto something, you think – you're always clutching at straws – this is what life is all about. I think artists are lucky because the straws are always blowing out of their hands. But the unfortunate thing is that most people find the straw hat and hang on to it, like your best

friend that got the job at the bank when he was 15 and looked 28 before he was 20. "Oh, this is it! Now I know what I'm doing! Right? Down the road for the next hundred years"...and it ain't never that. Whether it's a religious hat or a political hat or a no-political hat: whatever hat it was, always looking for these straw hats. I think I found out it's a waste of time. There is no hat to wear. Just keep moving around and changing clothes is the best. That's all that goes on: change. **John, June 1975**

I was in Bermuda again, and it suddenly hit me about what women represent to us, not as the sex object or the mother, but just their contribution. That's why you hear me muttering at the beginning (of 'Double Fantasy') to the other half of the sky, which is Chairman Mao's famous statement. That it is the other half. You know all this thing about man, woman, man, woman, is a joke, you know. Without each other, there ain't nothing. So it was like this sort of...my God, you know, it was a different viewpoint of what I'd felt about woman and I can't express it better than I said in the song. And it's for Yoko but it's to all women. **John, December 6, 1980**

Women's and Children's Liberation: It's just absolutely ridiculous but when you think it's such a beautiful statement, you know, what (Yoko) was saying is true, woman is still the nigger – there's only one, you can talk about blacks, you can talk about Jews, you can talk about the Third World, you can talk about everything, but underlying that whole thing, under the whole crust of it is the women and beneath them the children, as Dick Gregory said to us in 1969 in Denmark, "Children's liberation is the next movement." Because they have no rights whatsoever absolutely none, women have a certain amount but children is the next thing – children power – but the women will liberate the children. **John, December 6, 1980**

It's the men who've come a long way from even contemplating the idea of equality. But although there is this thing called the women's movement, society just took a laxative and they've just farted. They haven't really had a good shit yet. **John, September 1980**

Any male image is a father figure. There's nothing wrong with it until you give them the right to give you sort of a recipe for your life. What happens is somebody comes along with a good piece of truth. Instead of the truth being looked at, the person who brought it is looked at. The messenger is worshipped, instead of the message. So there would be Christianity, Mohammedanism, Buddhism, Confucianism, Marxism, Maoism – everything – it is always about a person and never about what he says.
John, September 1980

Watching the wheels? The whole universe is a wheel, right? Wheels go round and round. They're my own wheels, mainly. But, you know, watching myself is like watching everybody else. And I watch myself through my child, too. Then, in a way, nothing is real, if you break the word down. As the Hindus or Buddhists say, it's an illusion, meaning all matter is floating atoms, right?

It's Rashomon. We all see it, but the agreed-upon illusion is what we live in. And the hardest thing is facing yourself. It's easier to shout "Revolution" and "Power to the people" than it is to look at yourself and try to find out what's real inside you and what isn't, when you're pulling the wool over your own eyes. That's the hardest one.

I used to think that the world was doing it to me and that the world owed me something, and that either the conservatives or the socialists or the fascists or the communists or the Christians or the Jews were doing something to me; and when you're a teeny-bopper, that's what you think. I'm forty now. I don't think that any more, 'cause I found out it doesn't fucking work! The thing goes on anyway, and all you're doing is jacking off, screaming about what your mommy or daddy or society did, but one has to go through that. For the people who even bother to go through that – most assholes just accept what is and get on with it, right? – but for the few of us who did question what was going on...I have found out personally – not for the whole world! – that I am responsible for it, as well as them. I am part of them. There's no separation; we're all one, so in that respect, I look at it all and think, "Ah, well, I have to deal with me again in that way. What is real? What is the illusion I'm living or not living?" And I have to deal with it every day. The layers of the onion. But that is what it's all about. **John, December 5, 1980**

You make your own dream. That's The Beatles' story, isn't it? That's Yoko's story. That's what I'm saying now. Produce your own dream...I can't wake you up. I can't cure you. You can cure you.

It's fear of the unknown. The unknown is what it is. And to be frightened of it is what sends everybody scurrying around chasing dreams, illusions, wars, peace, love, hate, all that – it's all illusion. Unknown is what it is. Accept that it's unknown and it's plain sailing. Everything is unknown – then you're ahead of the game. That's what it is. Right? **John, September 1980**

It's a big wonderful world out there. And Yoko and I are going to explore it until we die. **John, 1975**

"Ob-la-di Ob-la-da life goes on…"

Family

Paul with his father, Jim McCartney.

Because of my attitude, all the other boys' parents, including Paul's father, would say, "Keep away from him." The parents instinctively recognised what I was, which was a trouble-maker, meaning I did not conform and I would influence their kids, which I did. I did my best to disrupt every friend's home I had.

OPPOSITE: George with his second wife Olivia.

John, September 1980

It probably is schmaltzy. I'm from that sort of family. We were very close, with aunties and uncles always coming in, sing-songs and parties. I saw John and Yoko last time I was in New York and I happened to mention for some reason our family sing-songs. He said he never had them. He didn't have the sort of family life I had. Yoko didn't either, she had to make appointments to see her dad. I now realise how lucky I am to have a close, loving family. **Paul, April 1976**

On Paul's Mother's Death: That was one of the things that brought John and I very close together. We used to actually talk about it, being 16 or 17. We actually used to know, not in a cynical way, but in a way that was accepting the reality of the situation, how people felt when they said, "How's your mother?" and we'd say "Well, she's dead." We almost had a sort of joke, we'd have to say, "It's all right, don't worry." We'd both lost our mothers. It was never really spoken about much; no-one really spoke about anything real. There was a famous expression: "Don't real on me, man." **Paul, October 1986**

I was always very well-mannered and polite. My dad brought me up to always tip my cap to my elders and I used to do it until I was about fourteen and I didn't wear a cap any more. Now I force myself not to tolerate people I don't like. If people do something which irritates me, I let them know about it. **Paul, 1980**

Paul & Linda, John & Yoko, Getting Married: I think we spurred each other into marriage. They were very strong together which left me out of the picture, so then I got together with Linda and we got our own kind of strength. I think again that they were a little bit peeved that we got married first. **Paul, October 1986**

Linda and I met in a club in London called the Bag of Nails, which was right about the time that the club scene was going strong in London. She was down there with some friends...I was in my little booth and she was in her little booth and we were giving each other the eye you know...About a year later (I realised I wanted to marry her) We both thought it a bit crazy at the time, and we also thought it would be a gas...

None of us realised what...it was like someone marrying Mick (Jagger), you don't realise...you know there's going to be a lot of fans who are going to hate it, but you still end up thinking, well, it's my life. I know a lot of rock & roll stars or just even show business people who will regulate their life to their image. It can mess you up a lot. **Paul, January 1979**

Paul with Jane Asher.

Public Criticism of Linda: It made us stronger, really; the thing I'm beginning to understand now about Linda was that we were just two people who liked each other and found a lot in common and fell in love, got married and found that we liked it. To the world, of course, she was the girl that Paul McCartney had married, and she was a divorcée, which didn't seem right. People preferred Jane Asher (Paul's first long-term girl friend). Jane Asher fitted. She was a better Fergie.

Linda wasn't a very good Fergie for me and people generally tended to disapprove of me marrying a divorcée and an American. That wasn't too clever. None of that made a bit of difference: I actually just liked her, I still do and that's all it's to do with.

I mean, we got married in the craziest clothes when I look back on it. We didn't even bother to buy her a decent outfit. I can see it all now; I can see why people were amazed that I'd put her in the group. At the time it didn't seem the least bit unusual. I even had quotes from Jagger saying, "Oh, he's got his old lady on stage man." **Paul, October 1986**

The McCartney family, left to right: Heather, Linda, James, Stella, Paul and Mary.

Kids and Fame: I don't think they're going to be crazed-out kids. But it is funny sometimes. I remember I was sitting in a field and Heather was leading Mary and a little baby on a pony and Mary just said to me, "You're Paul McCartney, aren't you?" When she's talking to me normally, she'll just call me Daddy. When there's company around, she knows I'm Paul McCartney, in inverted commas. **Paul, January 1979**

Heather, my eldest daughter, was well into punk. She knew too many of them for my liking. She went out with Billy Idol. Just what a father needs, his daughter going out with Billy Idol. Dear me. **Paul, 1990**

Love and Marriage: Well, we've been up, we've been down, we've been in love, we've been out of love – we've been every which way, you know? It's certainly not been as idyllic as it looks on the surface. It's a real marriage, believe me – as real as any other marriage. The bottom line is that we love each other, and what's more, we like each other. It sounds corny, but what else can I say? **Paul, January 1986**

I had a dream one night about my mother. She died when I was fourteen so I hadn't really heard from her in quite a while, and it was very good. It gave me some strength. In my darkest hour, Mother Mary comes to me. I don't know whether you've got parents that are still living, but if you do...I get dreams with John in, and my Dad. It's very nice because you meet them again. It's wondrous, it's like magic. **Paul, October 1986**

George on his Mother's Death: She'd got a tumour on the brain, but the doctor was an idiot and was saying, "There's nothing wrong with her, she's having some psychological trouble." When I went up to see her, she didn't even know who I was. I had to punch the doctor out, because in England the family doctor has to be the one to get the specialist. So he got the guy to look at her and she ended up in the neurological hospital.

The specialist said, "She could end up being a vegetable, but if it was my wife or mother, I'd do the operation" – which was a horrendous thing where they had to drill a hole in her skull. She recovered a little bit for about seven months. And during that period, my father, who'd taken care of her, had suddenly exploded with ulcers and was in the same hospital.

I was pretending to them that the other one was okay. Then running back and forth to do this record 'All Things Must Pass'. I wrote the song ('Deep Blue')...at home one exhausted morning with those major and minor chords. It's all filled with the frustration and gloom of going to these hospitals, and the feeling of disease that permeated the atmosphere. Not being able to do anything for suffering family or loved ones is an awful experience. **George, 1986**

Eric Clapton in Love with George's Wife, Patti: Eric's been a close friend of mine for years. I would rather (Patti) was with him than with some dope. We both loved Eric and still do. (Separating) was the best thing for us to do and we just should have done it much sooner. But I didn't have the problem with it, Eric had the problem. Every time I'd go see him, he'd really be hung up about it and I was saying, "Fuck it man, don't be apologising," and he didn't believe me. I was saying, "I don't care." **George, 1977**

George with his first wife, model Patti Boyd.

The point is to have a balance between inner life and the external. Again, with relationships it never works if one person is into it and the other isn't. It's difficult on both sides. Usually if a fellow is into smack his girlfriend has to leave him or get in on it herself. It's like that. In a way we all have desires. We must learn either to fulfil them or terminate them. If you can do that by being celibate and it's easy to handle, it's okay. You can lose certain desires you had when you were younger, but particularly with sex and drugs – you have to watch it: you can't go "oh well, I'll just have a bit and be fulfilled." It doesn't work that way. First you have a bit and then you want more and more. **George, 1975**

The Responsibility of Fatherhood: I stopped being as crazy as I used to be because I want this child to have a father a bit longer. Also with a child around I can realise what it was like to be my father. At the same time, you can relive certain aspects of being a child. You watch them and have all these flashbacks of when you were a kid. It somehow completes the generation thing. **George, 1988**

George with son Dhani and wife Olivia.

Giving his Son Values: I try to make him realise that not everyone lives in such a big house or has as much money as we do. That's a very difficult lesson to teach someone in his position, but we think we do a good job. **George, 1988**

George's son and The Beatles: You can't turn on the television without seeing something to do with The Beatles, can you? As I was just saying to somebody earlier, kids pick up on The Beatles through the old movie '*Yellow Submarine*'. See, I made a point of not saying anything about them to him. But by the time he was five he wanted to know how the piano part to 'Hey Bulldog' went, which completely threw me because I didn't understand where he'd heard a song like that. I haven't heard that myself really. Then I realised it was in '*Yellow Submarine*'. **George, 1988**

I think people change one another when they become husband and wife. He certainly seems happier than he was before. George and Olivia are very domesticated. They really vibrate on the same wavelength. **George's friend Mukunda, 1988**

Ringo and his first wife Maureen.

Ringo's Divorce: I was married and had a wonderful marriage. For me it was for life when we started. But then it comes to the point where it didn't work. So, you know, and you try all these different rooms, and "Let's do it for the children" and all that bullshit and, in the end, you have to look at it and say: "It's not working anyway."

"Why am I staying here? Why am I doing this? Why is she into that? She's probably into that 'cause I'm into this," and then it's the breakdown. And I'm northern, so once it's broken, I cut it off as fast as I can. It's just an attitude I have: once it's gone, it's gone. **Ringo, 1980**

Ringo Meeting Second Wife Barbara: Last spring we were on the *Caveman* set in Mexico for two and a half months just as friends. Then suddenly one Sunday evening – flashes of light! It clicked and we've been together ever since. **Ringo, April 1981**

I'm incredibly happy now. I had always believed in Prince Charming, if ever he came riding up on his charger. And Richard came. We'll get married, and that's it...happily ever after, all the rest. So now I'm into fairy tales. **Ringo's second wife, Barbara Bach, 1980**

To me, Ringo is definitely Richie. Ringo is the public figure, and Richie is the man I live with. You see, I really knew very little about The Beatles. I didn't follow them. My favourite musicians were Ray Charles and Aretha Franklin, but music just wasn't my thing. **Ringo's second wife, Barbara Bach, April 1981**

Ringo's Son and The Beatles Legacy: It means nothing to him really, or it didn't used to, and he was so into his own tastes, and now he's starting to play them (The Beatles) and he's picking out...I would never push him into anything, he just finds them – the records are there, so he puts them on. I'm

really pleased he likes some of them. The first thing, when he used to play
'Back In The USSR', we put that on a thousand times which he'd asked for so
we could all go around the room playing aeroplanes. So they associate not
with the track but with the sound effect. That was when he was a lot
younger. Now he's learning the recorder at school. We've got a piano at
home, he bashes it, I show him a chord. I think he will be a musician, in fact.

He wanted to form a group in school based on Alice Cooper. The only
problem they had was they all wanted to be Alice. And he went around the
house for a couple of weeks, him and Jay, with big black-eye make-up on.
That doesn't bother me...it's great, because I don't think I'd have been
allowed to do it. **Ringo, January 1974**

Ringo with his second
wife, actress Barbara
Bach.

As a child, I would say, "But this is going on!" and everybody would look at me as if I was crazy. I always was so psychic or intuitive or poetic or whatever you want to call it, that I was always seeing things in a hallucinatory way.

It was scary as a child, because there was nobody to relate to. Neither my auntie nor my friends nor anybody could ever see what I did. It was very scary and the only contact I had was reading about an Oscar Wilde or a Dylan Thomas or a Vincent van Gogh – all those books that my auntie had that talked about their suffering because of their visions. Because of what they saw, they were tortured by society for trying to express what they were. I saw loneliness. **John, September 1980**

Because of my attitude, all the other boys' parents, including Paul's father, would say, "Keep away from him." The parents instinctively recognised what I was, which was a trouble-maker, meaning I did not conform and I would influence their kids, which I did. I did my best to disrupt every friend's home I had. **John, September 1980**

I had an auntie and an uncle and a nice suburban home, thank you very much. Hear this, Auntie. She was hurt by a remark Paul made recently that the reason I am staying home with Sean now is because I never had a family life. It's absolute rubbish. There were five women who were my family. Five strong, intelligent women. Five sisters. One happened to be my mother.

My mother was the youngest. She just couldn't deal with life. She had a husband who ran away to sea and the war was on and she couldn't cope with

John with his mother
Julia in Liverpool, 1950.

me, and when I was four and a half, I ended up living with her elder sister...My mother was alive and lived a 15-minute walk away from me all my life. I saw her off and on. I just didn't live with her.
John, September 1980

John's Mother Dies: She got killed by an off-duty cop who was drunk after visiting my auntie's house where I lived. I wasn't there at the time. She was just at a bus stop. I was 16. That was another big trauma for me. I lost her twice. When I was five and I moved in with my auntie, and then when she physically died. That made me more bitter; the chip on my shoulder I had as a youth got really big then. I was just re-establishing the relationship with her and she was killed. **John, September 1980**

John and his First Marriage: My marriage to Cyn was not unhappy. But it was just a normal marital state where nothing happened and which we continued to sustain. You sustain it until you meet someone who suddenly sets you alight. **John, 1973**

John with his first wife Cynthia

John and His First Son: I'm just sort of a figure in the sky. But he's obliged to communicate with me, even when he probably doesn't want to. I'm not going to lie to Julian. Ninety percent of the people on this planet, especially in the

West, were born out of a bottle of whiskey on a Saturday night, and there was no intent to have children. So ninety percent of us – that includes everybody – were accidents. I don't know anybody else who was a planned child. All of us were "Saturday night specials." Julian is in the majority, along with me and everybody else. **John, September 1980**

As I said in an interview, with Julian my first child, I would come home and there'd be a twelve-year-old-boy there who I had no relationship with whatsoever. Now he's seventeen. I'm getting a relationship now because we can talk and…about music and whatever he's got into and girlfriends and that kind of stuff…I'd come back from Australia and he'd be a different size. I wouldn't even recognize how he looked half the time.
John, December 6, 1980

John with his son Julian, 1967.

John & Yoko's Relationship: It is a teacher-pupil relationship. That's what people don't understand. She's the teacher and I'm the pupil.
John, September 1980

Yoko met me before she met John. She turned up for a charity thing, she wanted manuscripts, any spare lyric sheet you had around. Ours tended to be on the backs of envelopes and to tell the truth I didn't want to give her any…So I said, "Look, my mate might be interested," and I gave her John's address, and I think that's how they first hooked up. **Paul, October 1986**

John Meeting Yoko at her Art Show: The owner whispered to her, "Let him hammer a nail in. You know, he's a millionaire. He might buy it." And finally she said, "Okay. You can hammer a nail in for five shillings." So smartass says, "Well, I'll give you an imaginary five shilling and hammer an imaginary nail in." And that's when we really met. That's when we locked eyes and she got it and I got it, and as they say in all the interviews we do, the rest is history. **John, 1975**

Yoko v. Beatles: You see I presumed that I would just be able to carry on and just bring Yoko into our life. But it seemed that I either had to be married to them or Yoko, and I chose Yoko, and I was right. **John, 1971**

There's nothing more important than our relationship, nothing. And we dig being together all the time. And both of us could survive apart, but what for? I'm not going to sacrifice love, real love, for any fuckin' whore or any friend, or any business, because in the end you're alone at night. **John, 1970**

It's just handy to fuck your best friend. That's what it is. And once I resolved the fact that it was a woman as well, it's all right. We go through the trauma of life and death every day, so it's not much of a worry about what sex we are any more. I'm living with an artist who's inspiring me to work. And, you know, Yoko is the most famous unknown artist. Everyone knows her name, but nobody knows what she does. **John, March 1971**

I don't know how it happened. I just realised that (Yoko) knew everything I knew, and more probably, and that was coming out of a woman's head. It just sort of bowled me over. It was like finding gold or something, to find somebody that you could go and get pissed with, and have exactly the same relationship as any mate in Liverpool you ever had. But you could go to bed with it, and it could stroke your head when you felt tired, sick or depressed. It could also be a mother. As she was talking to me I would get to such a level that I would be going higher and higher. When she'd leave, I'd go back into this sort of suburbia. Then I'd meet her again and my head would open like I was on an acid trip. **John.**

Yoko, John and Julian, 1969.

Yoko and The Beatles Breakup: I think, looking back you know, I understand there'd be four guys very close together and the women had been, you know, the old-fashioned type of female that we all know and love, you know, the one that was in the kitchen all the time, with the baby, and she never came to the sessions. And suddenly we were together all the time, you know. Sort of in a corner mumbling and giggling together and doing 'Two Virgins' and bags, and there were Paul, George and Ringo saying, "What the hell are they doing? What's happening to him?" And my attention completely went off them. Now it wasn't deliberate. It was just like I was so involved and so intrigued with what we were doing, that I...and then we'd look around and see that we weren't being approved.

But I understand how they felt, because if it had been Paul or George or Ringo that had fallen in love with somebody and got totally involved suddenly, it wasn't like, you know somebody...George coming and saying, "I'm going to work with Eric Clapton and the Band now, and screw you." It wasn't that kind of thing at all. It was just suddenly this involvement. **John, December 6, 1980**

Marrying Yoko in Gibraltar: We wanted to get married on a cross-channel ferry. That was the romantic part, when we went to Southampton and then we couldn't get on because she wasn't English and she couldn't get that Day Visa to go across and they said, "Anyway you can't get married. The captain's not allowed to do it any more." So we were in Paris and we were calling Peter Brown...and said, "We want to get married, where can we go?" And he called back and said, "Gibraltar's the only place." So – Okay, let's go. And we went there and it was beautiful. It's the pillar of Hercules. But they thought the world outside was the...a mystery from there, so that was like the Gateway to the World. So we liked it in the symbolic sense, and the Rock foundation of our relationship. **John, December 6, 1980**

On Leaving Yoko for Eighteen Months: One day I went out for a cup of coffee and some papers, and I didn't come back. **John, 1980**

(Yoko) kicked me out. Suddenly, I was on a raft alone in the middle of the universe. At first, I thought, Whoopee! Whoopee! You know, bachelor life! Whoopee! And then I woke up one day and I thought, What is this? I want to go home! But she wouldn't let me...she would say, "You're not ready to come home." So what do you say? OK, back to the bottle...It was the lost weekend that lasted 18 months. **John, September 1980**

Privacy and Family: No, we never decided to give up our private life. We decided that if we were going to do anything like get married, or like this film we are going to make now, that we would dedicate it to peace and the concept of peace...Peace is still important and my life is dedicated to living, just surviving is what it's about really, from day to day. **John, 1970**

Most people don't have a companion who will tell the truth and refuses to live with a bullshit artist, which I am pretty good at. I can bullshit myself and everybody around. Yoko: That's my answer. **John, September 1980**

John at a Tokyo Press Conference in 1977: We have basically decided, without a great decision, to be with our baby as much as we can until we feel we can take time off to indulge ourselves in creating things outside the family. **John, October 1977**

Sean Lennon in 1989.

(Yoko and I) learned that it's better for the family if we are both working for the family, she doing the business and me playing mother and wife. We re-ordered our priorities. The number-one priority is her and the family. Everything else revolves around that. **John, September 1980**

Yoko's Three Miscarriages: Yeah, enough to make us miserable about it, you know. Think we could never have a child. But we did. It turned out an English doctor told me, something wrong with my sperm, you know, because of the hard life I'd led. And he said I could never have a baby, that we could never have a baby because of me. But we met this Chinese acupuncturist in San Francisco. He said, "What about your wife? You have baby. Just be good boy. Eat well. No drugs. No drink." So that's what we did. And we had a baby. **John, December 6, 1980**

(Sean) is what they call a love child in truth. Doctors told us we could never have a child. We almost gave up. **John, September 1980**

Sean is not going to eat sugar and Sean is not going to watch TV commercials and people shooting each other and he's not gonna have the TV as a baby-sitter and he's not gonna go to school and he's not gonna be ignored and he's not gonna have his questions unanswered. **John, 1977**

The Beatles and Sean: I haven't said anything. Beatles were never mentioned to him. There was no reason to mention it; we never played Beatle records around the house...He did see *Yellow Submarine* at a friend's, so I had to explain what a cartoon of me was doing in a movie. **John, September 1980**

John on the Bliss of Domesticity: An incredible thing happened to me today...I baked my first loaf of bread and you can't believe how perfectly it rose, and I've taken a Polaroid picture of it and I think I can get it out to you (in L.A.) by messenger tonight. **John, 1977**

It's great the jokes, they did a thing on *Saturday Night Live* (American TV Programme), you know they had me in an apron and Yoko with a tie and all that, and they did a real good skit on us and we were hysterical, you know, I mean it was just very funny. All the time I kept saying, "Oh look the oven's burning" and that was the skit of me. I don't mind the mickey taking at all, because to me I approached it intellectually. First as a kind of Zen discipline, make the bed, conquered the rice, conquered the dependence on woman, even if I'm alone, I can now cook...enough to get by. **John, December 6, 1980**

Listen, if somebody's gonna impress me, whether it be a Maharishi or a Yoko Ono, there comes a point when the emperor has no clothes. There comes a point when I will see. So for all you folks out there who think that I'm having the wool pulled over my eyes, well, that's an insult to me. Not that you think less of Yoko, because that's your problem. What I think of her is what counts! Because – fuck you, brother and sister – you don't know what's happening. I'm not here for you, I'm here for me and the baby!
John, September 1980

"I Am The Walrus"

On Themselves

I have nothing to prove any more you know. I am the best rock & roll drummer in the world. What else can I do? Ringo, January 1991

You can't stay angry forever, twenty years after an event that hurt. Time is a great healer. **Paul, February 1990**

You're constantly trying to remember if you're OK or not. I hate justifying myself. I remember asking George Martin once, George, are we really gonna have to keep justifying ourselves? He said, "Yeah. Forever..." **Paul, July 1989**

Producer George Martin with Paul.

I know The Beatles used to say, "We won't be rock & rollin' when we're forty," but I still love it. **Paul, January 1986**

It's like if you've been an astronaut and you've been to the moon, what do you do with the rest of your life. **Paul, 1990**

After you've gone through the whole bit of performing and showing everyone how famous you are, you realise you don't need to show anyone any more. **Paul, April 1970**

I sometimes hear myself in interviews going, Well I'm just a sort of ordinary guy. And I think, Will they go away thinking, Did he really say he was an ordinary guy? 'Cos there's a lot of evidence to the contrary. **Paul, July 1989**

I'd put me at the top. Just because I'm a competitor, man. You don't have Ed Moses going around saying, "Sure, I'm the third-best hurdler in the world." You don't find Mike Tyson saying, "Sure, there's lots of guys who could beat me." You've got to slog, man. I've slogged my way from the suburbs of Liverpool, and I am not about to put all that down. **Paul, August 1990**

I don't actually want to be a living legend. I came into this to get out of having a job, and to pull birds. And I pulled quite a few birds, and got out of having a job, so that's where I am still. It's turned out to be very much a job, a bloody hard job the way I do it, running a company and stuff, but I do like it. **Paul, July 1989**

You can easily lose your identity in this sort of business. You confuse the myth with the person you really are. Like Marilyn Monroe must have got to the point where she didn't know who she was any more. She was a walking legend, not a person. And because she was a legend, she had to be kind and patient to every little creep who ever pestered her. I make sure that being well known doesn't stop me being an ordinary bloke who won't tolerate people he doesn't like. **Paul, 1980**

There's one thing about sudden death. There are so many things left unsaid. I was really worried for a few weeks afterwards. There are crazy people everywhere. But I really couldn't live like that (under guard). My attitude is to

Paul and Linda with their son James, 1982.

try and push it out of my mind. I would just like to have seen John the day before (he died) and straightened everything out with us. We found we could talk to each other as long as it was about kids, and stuff like that. **Paul, 1984**

It's like when people used to talk about living in the shadow of The Bomb. Well it's true, but what good does it do to think like that? You've just got to get on with it. We're all in the shadow of something, and I'm not the only person out there who might get mugged or might get shot at. **Paul, July 1989**

I think that I've got a certain personality and if I give charity I don't like to shout about it. If I get into avant-garde stuff, I don't particularly shout about that either. I just get on with it. **Paul, October 1986**

I do think John's avant-garde period later, was really to give himself a go at what he'd seen me going at. Because I talk about this so much, people go around saying, "Oh, he's trying to reclaim The Beatles for himself, to take it away from John." I'm not doing anything of the kind. I'm not trying to claim the history and achievements of The Beatles for myself. I'm just trying to reclaim my part of it.

It's not sour grapes. It's true. I was there in the mid-Sixties when all these things started to happen in London. The Indica Gallery art people like Robert Fraser. I was living in London, and I was the only bachelor of the four. The others were married and living in the suburbs. I was just there when it all started to happen.

The difference is that once John got interested in it, he did it like everything else – to extremes. He did it with great energy and enthusiasm. He drove into it head-first with Yoko. So it looked like he had been the one doing all the avant-garde stuff.

It's the ultimate conundrum. If I don't say anything, I go on being the so-called wimp of the group. If I do open my mouth, it looks like I'm sullying John. **Paul, February 1990**

Songwriting: Sometimes you've only got an airline sickbag to write it on, hotel notepaper, backs of envelopes, toilet paper. It's been done on everything, you know. So it's just an adventure every time I do it. **Paul, 1990**

As a kid, when depressed I would go off with the guitar, often to the bathroom, because it had the best acoustics, and hold the guitar to myself. That's one of my little hammy theories, incidentally – a guitar you hold to you, like another body: a piano you push away from you – they're two different physical acts. **Paul, December 1990**

There's not much that takes years and years. If it takes that long I normally abort it...The best songs are normally written in one go. They're just done, inspiration just comes quickly, it falls in place. Something like 'Put It There' was done very quickly while I was on holiday. **Paul, 1990**

Somehow there is a rather funny image of me, even though on my solo albums I played everything. 'McCartney' still wasn't called: "The album

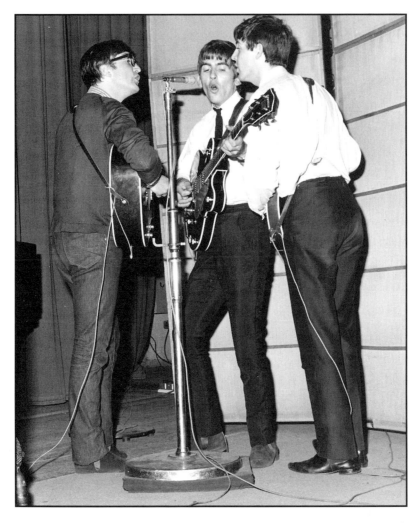

where he plays everything." It was all done subtly. Rather coy. I always do things a bit coy, because I'd rather that than be too showy and have it not come off. I know I can do it and have confidence in myself. **Paul, 1984**

I always suggested to Ringo things that he might play. I hear drums well. I first got into them listening to 'Sweet Little Sixteen'. I'd ask Ringo to play a variation on those sort of drum breaks. At sessions I'd just climb on the drum kit and start having a go. I got the feeling I could do it as long as nothing difficult was required. **Paul, 1984**

I've been composing melodies long enough to understand the mechanics of it. I just can't notate and I don't want to learn to. It's almost a superstition. **Paul, December 1990**

I've already done the thing where you go out and shun The Beatles. That was Wings. Now I've done this whole thing (The 1990 World Tour). I recognize that I'm a composer and that those Beatles songs are a part of my material.

The only alternative is for me to turn my back on it forever, never do 'Hey Jude' again – and I think it's a damn good song. It would really be a pity if I don't do it. Because someone else will. **Paul, February 1990**

I'm a Beatles fan. When John was saying a couple of years ago that it was all crap, it was all a dream, I know what he was talking about, but at the same time I was sitting here thinking, "No it wasn't." **Paul, 1976**

You can't get it right all the time. If there's been a fault with my stuff, I think some of it was unfinished. Looking back on some of it now, I think "You didn't finish a bloody thing." So...yeah, I might have been a bit soft (after leaving The Beatles), and some of it might have been a bit unfinished. **Paul, January 1986**

I just think of myself as a hack writer. People just ring up. Rod Stewart rang me up and asked me to write a song for him so I did 'Mine For Me' for his album. Then they asked me to write the theme for the James Bond movie (*Live And Let Die*). The idea just has to appeal to me and I'll do it. I don't like to feel that I'm a "major influence on the music scene." I don't believe that. **Paul, 1984**

What I really want for myself is the freedom to play to 56,000 people and be able to manage that and the next night go and play a pub somewhere. **Paul, 1984**

You can't win them all. I've done so much, there has to be an element that doesn't make it. I don't know how many songs I've written, but I have had a fair share of success. **Paul, July 1989**

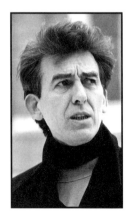

I feel pretty good about it. I feel amazed that I can still sing, 'cos I'm 46, I never expected to be doing this when I was 46. We used to think that 25 was the end of the line. I really do get off on doing it. Jamming is what I really love. Who'd have ever thought I'd still be messing around with electric guitars? **Paul, July 1989**

Is it a priority to go around being a rock and roll star? There's no time to lose really. There are lots of times I've been heavily into it and then other times I come right back out of it. There are a lot of people in this business that I love, friends, who are really great but who don't have any desire for knowledge or realization. It's good to boogie once in a while, but when you boogie all your life away, it's just a waste of a life and of what we've been given. **George, 1975**

George, after losing the 'My Sweet Lord' copyright case: I've written enough songs now so whatever they say, I'm cool, I know the motive behind writing the song and I don't feel guilty about it all. **George, 1980**

If you're into the songwriting mood, then anything can trigger it. I had these three friends who were all in AA (Alcoholics Anonymous) at my house one night back in 1983, and this guy showed me a brochure that was called *Just For Today*. It seemed so nice to try and live through this day only. I mean, it's not just for alcoholism. It's good for everybody to remember that we can only live today and the only thing that exists is now. The past is gone, the future we don't know about. So it's like an extension of the "be here now" idea. I thought it would make a nice song, so I wrote it. **George, 1988**

We (Paul, George & Ringo) have been having dinner together. We are friends now; it's the first time we have been this close for a long time. But it doesn't mean to say that we are going to make another group or anything. You know, I could go out and try to be a superstar, and I tell you, if I went to an agent and a manager, and checked myself out and practised a bit, I could do it. But I don't really want to do that. That's being a kamikaze pop star, the tours and everything. I don't have to prove anything...I don't want to be in the business full-time because I'm a gardener: I plant flowers and watch them grow. **George, 1989**

Ringo with Rory Storm
and The Hurricanes,
Butlins Holiday Camp,
Skegness, 1961.

Ringo was a star in his own right in Liverpool before we even met...He would
have surfaced with or without The Beatles. **John, September 1980**

I never studied anything, really. I didn't study drums. I joined bands and
made all the mistakes onstage. I feel I learn more from professionals than
from going to school. I don't particularly want to go to a class when I can get
up with someone who knows his gig and can teach me. I learned a lot from
some fine actors, like Richard Burton and Peter Sellers. I feel that was the best
"school" I ever went to. **Ringo, April 1980**

I'm always good for starting a bit of a tune and the first verse, but after that I
just can never go anywhere. It takes me years, that's why I'm so slow.
Ringo, January 1974

I'm most creative as a drummer. I'm probabiy the best rock & roll drummer
on earth. I say that now because I used to be embarrassed to speak for myself.
I was often ignored because John and Paul were songwriters, and then George
started writing. I wrote my little songs too, but I didn't write anything to
compare with theirs. 'Don't Pass Me By' was the first track I ever wrote that
was recorded. That was my song. But imagine, I was in this band with the
greatest songwriters on earth at the time! I used to fetch in my little songs,
and they'd all have hysterics because all I was doing was writing new words
to old tunes. They'd be on the floor laughing! So I had to get to the point
where I could say I'd written a definite song – something that was not a
rewrite of a Jerry Lee Lewis song. **Ringo, April 1981**

For me, the groove is three, five, 15 guys in a studio just getting it on
together. It's just really good, and you all know when it's good. And you all
know when it's bad, but sometimes you've had enough and you're saying,
"Oh, that's all right." We used to do that. We'd be fed up at the end of the
night, we'd say, "Yeah, yeah, that's it," and we'd come back the next day and
do it all again. Because we knew. **Ringo, January 1974**

What I have to combat is the original image of me as the downtrodden dummy. It's still on everybody's minds. You don't know how hard it is to fight that tag. I've been caught in this trap for almost twenty years now. But it hasn't ruined my life. I know what I am. I know what I can do. But what am I going to do, take a newspaper ad or a billboard and say, "I'm not really like that?" **Ringo, April 1981**

We can all do so many things...and I'm so lucky anyway, just being in the position I ended up in by joining this little band...you're allowed to do anything. If I was still with Nicky and the Red Streaks up in Liverpool they would never allow me to try and act or design furniture or write things...you're not allowed, it's funny. It's like when you've got no bread no one gives you a drum kit, but when you're making it...I've got five kits. I can buy my own now but they give me them. I suppose that's the way of the world. **Ringo, January 1974**

I look at early pictures of myself, and I was torn between being Marlon Brando and being the sensitive poet – the Oscar Wilde part of me with the velvet, feminine side. I was always torn between the two, mainly opting for the macho side, because if you showed the other side, you were dead. **John, December 5, 1980**

I was just a suburban kid, imitating the rockers. But it was a big part of one's life to look tough. I spent the whole of my childhood with shoulders up around the top of me head and me glasses off because me glasses were sissy, and walking with complete fear, but with the toughest little face you've ever seen. **John, December 5, 1980**

I'm often afraid, and I'm not afraid to be afraid. But it's more painful to try not to be yourself. People spend a lot of time trying to be somebody else, and I think it leads to terrible diseases...I think it has something to do with constantly living or getting trapped in an image or an illusion of themselves, suppressing some part of themselves whether it's the feminine side or the fearful side. **John, December 5, 1980**

I've never claimed divinity. I've never claimed purity of soul. I've never claimed to have the answer to life. I only put out songs and answer questions as honestly as I can, but only as honestly as I can – no more, no less. I cannot live up to other people's expectations of me because they're illusionary. And the people who want more than I am, or than Bob Dylan is, or than Mick Jagger is... **John, December 5, 1980**

You don't have to be trained in rock and roll to be a singer; I didn't have to be trained as a singer: I can sing. Singing is singing to people who enjoy what you're singing, not being able to hold notes – I don't have to be in rock and roll to create. When I'm an old man, (Yoko and I) will make wallpaper together, but just to have the same depth and impact. The message is the medium. **John, 1970**

Creating is the result of pain, too. I have to put it somewhere and I write songs. **John, 1970**

I want people to love me. I want to be loved. **John, 1970**

What do you want to be? What are you lookin' for? And that's about it. I'm a freakin' artist, man, not a fuckin' racehorse. **John, 1970**

You see I'm shy and aggressive, so I have great hopes for what I do with my work and I also have great despair that it's all pointless and it's shit. How can you beat Shakespeare or Beethoven or whatever? I go through all that, and in my secret heart I wanted to write something that would take over 'We Shall Overcome'. **John, 1970**

Sexist Pig: I am the one who has come a long way. I was the pig. And it is a relief not to be a pig. The pressures of being a pig were enormous.
John, September 1980

All music is rehash. There are only a few notes. Just variations on a theme.
John, September 1980

I'm okay. I'm not technically very good, but I can make it fucking howl and move. I was rhythm guitarist. It's an important job. I can make a band drive.
John, 1970

I'm really very embarrassed about my guitar playing in one way because it's very poor. I can never move, but I can make a guitar speak, you know.
John, 1970

On Fame: I just got myself in a party, I was emperor, I had millions of chicks, drugs, drink, power and everybody saying how great I was. How could I get out of it? It was just like being in a fuckin' train. I couldn't get out.

I couldn't create either. I created a little, it came out, but I was in the party and you don't get out of things like that. It was fantastic! I came out of the sticks, I didn't hear about anything – Van Gogh was the most far-out thing I'd ever heard of. Even London was something we used to dream of, and London's nothing. I came out of the fuckin' sticks to take over the world it seemed to me, I was enjoying it, and I was trapped in it, too. I couldn't do anything about it, I was just going along for the ride. I was hooked, just like a junkie. **John, 1970**

The unfortunate thing about egomaniacs is that they don't take much attention to other people's work. I only assess people on whether they are a danger to me or my work or not. **John, 1970**

People like me are aware of their so-called genius at ten, eight, nine...I always wondered, "Why has nobody discovered me?" In school, didn't they see that I'm cleverer than anybody in this school? That the teachers are stupid, too? That all they had was information that I didn't need.

I used to get fuckin' lost being in high school. I used to say to my auntie, "You throw my fuckin' poetry out and you'll regret it when I'm famous," and she threw the bastard stuff out.

I never forgave her for not treating me like a fuckin' genius or whatever I was, when I was a child. **John, 1970**

Nobody says it, so you scream it: "look at me, a genius, for fuck's sake! What do I have to do to prove to you son-of-a-bitches what I can do, and who I am? Don't dare, don't you dare fuckin' dare criticise my work like that. You, who don't know anything about it. Fuckin' bullshit." **John, 1970**

Yoko and I have clashed artistically. Our egos have smashed once or twice. But if I know what I'm doing as an artist, then I can see if I'm being hypocritical in my reactions. I sometimes am overawed by her talent. I think, fuck, I better watch out, she is taking over, I better get myself in here.
John, April 1971

Politics and John's Music: It almost ruined it, in a way. It became journalism and not poetry. And I basically feel that I'm a poet. Even if it does go "ba-deedle, eedle, eedle, it, da-deedle, deedle, it." I'm not a formalised poet, I have no education so I have to write in the simplest forms usually...I realised that we were poets but we were really folk poets, and Rock & Roll was folk music...You get into that bit where you can't talk about trees, 'cause, y'know, y'gotta talk about "Corruption on Fifty-fourth Street"! It's nothing to do with that. It's a bit larger than that. **John, June 1975**

The Sixties: Whatever wind was blowing at the time moved The Beatles, too. I'm not saying we weren't flags on the top of a ship; but the whole boat was moving. Maybe The Beatles were in the crow's nest, shouting, "Land ho," or something like that, but we were all in the same damn boat.
John, September 1980

I don't want to grow up but I'm sick of not growing up...I'll find a different way of not growing up. There's a better way of doing it than torturing your body. And then your mind. The guilt! It's just so dumb. And it makes me furious to be dumb because I don't like dumb people. And there I am doing the dumbest things...I seem to do the things that I despise the most, almost. All of that to – what? – avoid being normal.

John and Yoko with assorted friends and musicians including George (left), Lyceum, London, 1969.

John performs 'I Saw Her Standing There' during the Elton John concert at Madison Square Garden, New York, 1973.

I have this great fear of this normal thing. You know, the ones that passed their exams, the ones that went on to their jobs, the ones that didn't become rock & rollers, the ones that settled for it, settled for it, settled for the deal! That's what I'm trying to avoid. But I'm sick of avoiding it with violence, you know? I've gotta do it some other way. I think I will. I think just the fact I've realised it is a good step forward. Alive in '75 is my new motto. I've just made it up. That's the one. I've decided I want to live. I'd decided I wanted to live before, but I didn't know what it meant, really. It's taken however many years and I want to have a go at it. **John, June 1975**

On Being Harassed by the U.S. Government in the Early 1970s: You know, (Yoko and I) seem to just go ploughing on any way producing it, but still I wonder how it would have been had we not been harassed, but one cannot always blame everything on the outside. Whatever happened to us was also partly our creation. And it was probably to do with complete self-involvement and not really taking care of business on an outside level and looking where we were going. **John, December 6, 1980**

I've had tongue in cheek all along. 'I am the Walrus', all of them had tongue in cheek, you know, I don't, just because other people see depths of whatever in it, you know, what does it really mean "I am the Eggman"? It could have been the pudding basin for all I cared. It was just tongue in cheek, it's not that serious. **John, December 6, 1980**

Looking back at it, whenever I comment about writing, I always seem to have been suffering, whether it was writing 'Day In The Life' or whatever, when I comment about it, everything is like some kind of suffering. I always seem to have an intense time writing and thinking this is the end and nothing's coming and this is dumb and how can I, this is no good and all that business. **John, December 6, 1980**

Song-Writing With Paul: You could say that (Paul) provided a lightness, an optimism, while I would always go for the sadness, the discords, a certain bluesy edge. **John, September 1980**

Missing Paul: I never actually felt a loss. I don't want it to sound negative, like I didn't need Paul, because when he was there, obviously, it worked. But I can't – it's easier to say what I gave to him than what he gave to me. And he'd say the same. **John, September 1980**

It was fun, sometimes it's fun but then it gets to be stupid, that's why I started from the 'Mother' album onwards trying to shave off all imagery, pretensions of poetry, illusions of grandeur, I call à la Dylan Dylanesque. I didn't write any of that. Just say what it is, simple English, make it rhyme and put a backbeat on it and express yourself as simply as possible, straightforwardly as possible. **John, December 6, 1980**

I've got used to the fact that whatever I do is going to be compared to the other Beatles. If I took up ballet dancing, my ballet dancing would be compared to Paul's bowling. So that I'll have to live with. But I've come to learn something big this past year. I cannot let the Top Ten dominate my art. If my worth is only to be judged by whether I'm in the Top Ten or not, then I'd better give up. Because if I let the Top Ten dominate my art, then the art will die. **John, 1974**

On not Playing in Public for Five Years: Well, it wasn't a matter of resisting. The first half year or year that I had this sort of feeling in the back of my mind that I ought to, and I'd go through periods of panic when...because I was not in the *NME (New Musical Express)* or the *Billboard Magazine* or being seen at Studio 54 with Mick (Jagger) and Bianca...I mean I just didn't exist any more. I got a little fear that would come on like paranoia, then it would go away because I'd be involved with the baby or involved with whatever sort of business we were involved with. But that only lasted about

John, with Yoko, adopting his 'respectable' image while awaiting his US visa in New York during the seventies.

nine months, and then there was suddenly like a "oh!" it just went away, and I realised there was a life after death, you know, there was a life without it.

It was great, it was like, oh my God, and I would sit around thinking what does this remind me of, what does this remind me of? It reminds me of being fifteen. I didn't have to write songs at fifteen. I wrote if I wanted to but played Rock 'n' Roll if I wanted to. I didn't have to do it, I didn't have some imaginary standard set up by me or by some group of critics or whatever.
John, December 6, 1980

Playing Again, After Five Years: You breathe in and you breathe out. (Yoko and I) feel like doing it, and we have something to say. Also, Yoko and I attempted a few times to make music together, but that was a long time ago and people still had the idea that The Beatles were some kind of sacred thing that shouldn't step outside its circle. It was hard for us to work together then. We think either people have forgotten or they have grown up by now, so we can make a second foray into that place where she and I are together, making music – simply that. It's not like I'm some wondrous, mystic prince from the rock & roll world dabbling in strange music with this oriental dragon lady, which was the picture projected by the press before. **John, September 1980**

You can't be discussing it while you're making it...And it's only when you look back at it, you...oh, I see what I was feeling at the time, even though one tries to express it in the music, you're not conscious of what you're expressing; and it's sometimes about two or three years later when I've realised what we made them. But 'Double Fantasy' I can talk all night about it, but it'll be two years before I can see it really, what it is.
John, December 6, 1980

Living in New York: I would be walking around tense like, waiting for somebody to say something, or jump on me, and it took me two years to unwind. I can go right out this door now and go into a restaurant. You know how great that is? Or go to the movies? I mean people come and ask for autographs or say, Hi, but they don't bug you, you know. They just – Oh, hey, how you doin',? Like your record. Because we got a record out now, but before they'd shout, How you doin? You know. How's the baby? Oh, great thanks. **John, December 6, 1980**

"When I'm Sixty-Four..."

John & the Future

It looks like I'm going to be 40 and life begins at 40 – so they promise. And I believe it, too. I feel fine and I'm very excited. It's like, you know, hitting 21, like, "Wow, what's going to happen next?" John, September 1980

LEFT: John and Yoko on the streets of New York, 1980.

The 1980s: I think it's going to be the one period they say, Those two will do anything for publicity, for Christ's sake get them off the front pages, oh get them off. People are bitching at us because we were always doing something; and then they were bitching at us because we weren't doing anything. And I have this funny feeling that it's going to be the other way around again, because we're talking and talking and talking and all sorts of plans and ideas we have in our heads, it's all a matter of getting it done, you know? We already got half the next album, and we'll probably go in after Christmas and do that. And we're already talking about the ideas for the third album. It is already laid out and I can't wait, you know. **John, December 6, 1980**

The game isn't over yet. Everyone talks in terms of the last record or the last Beatle concert – but God willing, there are another 40 years of productivity to go. I'm not judging whether 'I Am The Walrus' is better or worse than 'Imagine'. It is for others to judge. I am doing it. I do. I don't stand back and judge – I do. **John, September 1980**

I never see myself as not an artist. I never let myself believe that an artist can "run dry."

I've always had this vision of bein' sixty and writing children's books. I don't know why. **John, June 1975**

It's better to fade away like an old soldier than to burn out. **John, September 1980**

Floral tributes to John left by fans at the front gate of the Dakota Building directly after his assassination.

When I'm 64: I hope we're a nice old couple living off the coast of Ireland or something like that – looking at our scrap-book of madness. **John, 1970**

"The walrus was Paul..."

On Each Other

They are my brothers, you see. I'm an only child, and they're my brothers. I've always said that if I ever spend all my bread, I can just go and live with one of them, and vice versa, 'cause we all love to spend it.
Ringo, April 1981

I had a great day the other day when George came down to visit me and for the first time in billions of years we had a really nice time. George was my original mate in The Beatles...We'd got all professional and Beatles and everything, and you lose that obviously, and he just came down the other day and we didn't talk about Apple and we didn't touch an instrument. It was just back as mates. **Paul, October 1986**

We're all kind of coming to. We all brushed off the whole Beatles episode and sort of said, Well it's no big deal...it was a huge deal...if there ever was a big deal, that was it! So I don't think half of us know what happened to us really. I can never tell you what year anything was; literally they all go into a haze for me, the years and stuff. **Paul, October 1986**

John was lucky. He got all his hurt out. I'm a different sort of personality. There's still a lot inside me that's trying to work it out. **Paul, October 1986**

(John) was one great guy, but part of his greatness was that he wasn't a saint. **Paul, October 1986**

Looking back on it with John, you know, he was a really great guy. I always idolised him. We always did, the group. I don't know if the others will tell you that, but he was our idol. **Paul, November 1987**

Paul, Linda, Olivia, Barbara and Ringo at London's Hippodrome following the London première of *Give My Regards To Broad Street*, 1984.

(John) had periods when he renounced the whole thing, and I remember him phoning me to say, "Look lad, it's the most difficult thing to renounce our fame because we're so hooked on fame, but it's great, you should kick it over!" And I'm going, Hmmm, do tell me. **Paul, July 1989**

The great thing about me and John is that it was me and John. End of story. That's the one great thing I can think, whereas everyone else can say so-and-so, so-and-so. That's the nice thing. When we got in a little room it was me and John sitting there, it was me and him who wrote it, not all these other people who think they know all about it. It was me. I must know better than them, I was in the room with him. **Paul, July 1989**

Maybe we should have taken to Yoko a little better. I often do feel not too clever about not talking to her, because we didn't get on too well. She was very different from anything we'd encountered. A lot of people still find her a little difficult to take. I figure, well, he loved her, so it's nothin' to do with me – I should respect her through him. And I felt that I tried to do that. But we were being so set against each other that his unreasonable bitterness was almost inevitable, I think. It's such a pity he felt that way. But the bottom line is we loved each other. And I'm glad to be getting back to some semblance of sanity with George and Ringo now – we can meet and hug and say we love each other, you know? **Paul, January 1986**

I was trying to exorcise the demons in my own head, 'cos it's fairly tough when you have someone like John slagging you off in public, 'cos he's a fairly tough slagger-offer. Like he said my singing was like Engelbert Humperdinck, which I quoted somewhere, and Engelbert rang up, he got really annoyed. He thought I'd originated it, and I said, "No, John said it, about me." And he says, "John Lennon would have never said that." **Paul, July 1989**

Paul on John's Criticism: Oh, I hated it. You can imagine, I sat down and pored over every little paragraph, every little sentence. "Does he really think that of me?" And at the time, I thought, "It's me. That's just what I'm like. He's captured me so well; I'm a turd, you know."

I sat down and really thought, I'm just nothin'. But then, well, kind of people who dug me like Linda said, "Now you know that's not true, you're joking. He's got a grudge, man; the guy's trying to polish you off." Gradually I started to think, great, that's not true. I'm not really like Engelbert; I don't just write ballads. And that kept me kind of hangin' on; but at the time, I tell you, it hurt me. Whew. Deep. **Paul, January 1974**

Paul on John's Rock Sabbatical: People are calling John a recluse because he isn't doing what they expect him to do. In fact he's been getting on with being a family man. He's cooking and having a great time. **Paul, 1979**

What I cherish is that, apart from the venomous period, I know that I sat there and we wrote 'Love Me Do'. And I sat there and we wrote 'I Want To Hold Your Hand', and we screwed around with the lyrics. I know he brought in 'In My Life', and he had the first verse and the rest of it wasn't written. And I know he brought in 'Norwegian Wood' and we developed the idea of setting the place on fire. I remember sitting there doing 'Help!', and then I'd come in with "When I was younger, so much younger than today," and he'd have the main melody, and I'd do the counter melody. I can remember where we were, how it was and just magic moments where I'd be writing, "It's getting better all the time," and John would be sitting there – "It can't get much worse." Those moments. That's what I cherish. No one can take it away from me. **Paul, November 1987**

I was one of the biggest friends in his life, one of the closest people to him. I can't claim to be the closest, although it's possible. It's contentious, but I wouldn't...I don't need the credit. **Paul, November 1987**

John's Sudden Death: It was crazy. It was anger. It was fear. It was madness. It was the world coming to an end. **Paul, 1984**

When John was killed, somebody stuck a microphone (in my face) and said, "What do you think about it?" I said, "It's a drag." But I said, "It's a dra-a-a-ag," and meant it with every inch of melancholy I could muster. When you put that in print, it says, "McCartney in London today, when asked for a comment on his dead friend, said, 'It's a drag.'" It seemed a very flippant comment to make.

Then the pundits come on. "Yes, so John was the bright one in the group. Yes, he was a very clever one. Oh, well, he'll be sorely missed, and he was a great so-and-so." I said, "Bloody hell, how can you muster such glib things?" But they were the ones who came off good, because they said suitably meaningful things. I was the idiot who said, "It's a drag."
Paul, November 1987

Paul's Official Statement on John's Death: He was a great man and will be missed by the whole world and will be remembered for his art, music and contribution to world peace. **Paul, 1980**

I have hidden myself in my work today (December 9, 1980). But it keeps flashing into my mind. I feel shattered, angry, and very, very sad. It's just ridiculous. He was pretty rude about me sometimes, but I secretly admired him for it and I always managed to stay in touch with him. There was no question that we weren't friends – I really loved the guy.

I think that what has happened will in years to come make people realise that John was an international statesman. He often looked a loony to many people. He made enemies, but he was fantastic. He was a warm man who cared a lot and, with the record 'Give Peace A Chance', he helped stop the Vietnam war – he made a lot of sense. **Paul, 1980**

People say we were worlds apart but we weren't. We actually did know each other. We were actually very close. We had a ding dong in the press especially after the Apple stuff. Yoko told me how very complimentary he was about me, but he just didn't want to be the cloying, sycophantic sort of guy saying in public, "Oh Paul's terrific – he's really great."

There was a very competitive thing between us. Yoko says a lot of the slagging off was John taking the mickey. I talked to Yoko the day after he was killed and the first thing she said was, "John was really fond of you." He was very jealous and so was I. The last telephone call I had with him we were still the best of mates. **Paul, 1984**

Actually it was really nice, after John died, Yoko was quite kind in telling me that he did really love me, because it looked like he didn't.
Paul, November 1987

It's still weird even to say, "before he died." I still can't come to terms with that. I still don't believe it. It's like, you know, these dreams you have, where he's still alive; then you wake up and..."Oh." **Paul, January 1986**

It was all so tragic. But I do feel thankful that the last few years of his life were very happy, from what I can gather. He was always a very warm guy, John. His bluff was all on the surface. He used to take his glasses down – those granny glasses – take 'em down and say, "It's only me." They were like a wall, you know? A shield. Those are the moments I treasure. I suppose we hurt each other and stuff, but I keep looking at all the evidence of how I hurt him, and I don't know – it doesn't seem quite as bad as he was making it.
Paul, January 1986

The Mythologising of John: He never wanted that for himself. I remember driving in a car, listening to an interview with John on the radio on the day he died in which he said, "I don't want to be a martyr." He didn't want that responsibility, to be larger than life, to be some kind of god.
Paul, August 1990

The fact is we were a team, despite everything that went on between us and around us. And I was the only songwriter he ever chose to work with. Nuff said. **Paul, August 1990**

You'd read all these stories (told by John) – and they'd keep coming all the time – about how The Beatles weren't actually anything. That they didn't mean a thing. That he was the only one who had a clue about anything – and the wife. There was a definite strained relationship right from the 'White Album'. There was a lot of alienation between us and him.

There was alienation amongst all of us. It was particularly strained because having been in a band from being kids, then suddenly we're all grown up and we've got these other wives. That didn't exactly help. All the wives at that time really drove wedges between us. And then, after years, when I saw John in New York, it was almost like he was crying out to tell me certain things or to renew things, relationships, but he wasn't able to, because of the situation he was in. **George, November 1987**

The period when he was cooking bread and stuff, I always got an overpowering feeling from him. Almost a feeling that he wanted to say much more than he could, or than he did. You could see it in his eyes. But it was difficult. **George, November 1987**

The very first time we took LSD, John and I were together. And that experience together, and a lot of other things that happened after that, both on LSD and on the meditation trip in Rishikesh – we saw beyond each other's physical bodies, you know. That's there permanently, whether he's in a physical body or not. I mean this is the goal anyway: to realise the spiritual side. If you can't feel the spirit of some friend who's been that close, then what chance have you got of feeling the spirit of Christ or Buddha or whoever else you may be interested in? "If your memory serves you well, we're going to meet again." I believe that. **George, November 1987**

(Paul) should work with various other people and hopefully he'll find somebody who will actually tell him something because most people who work with Paul are afraid to say anything to him. And I think that's no good. You need to have somebody you can work with who'll tell you you're no good when you're no good. Otherwise, it's no help at all. **George, 1988**

For the last few years I've spoken my mind to (Paul) Whenever I felt something, like *'Broad Street'*, which I thought was a big mistake. Not making the film, because I quite enjoyed it myself, but the idea of trying to write everything yourself. That's the mistake. I think the only barrier between us now is our astrological signs. Some of the time we get on pretty well and the rest of the time I find that I really don't have anything in common with him. **George, 1988**

I think if you have a relationship with somebody else, you have to be able to trust each other, and to do that you have to be able to talk to each other straight. The thing with Paul is one minute he says one thing and he's really charming, and the next minute, you know, he's all uptight. Now we all go through that, good and bad stuff, but I think by now that we've got to find somewhere in the centre. Anyway, he's getting better. *'Broad Street'*, I think, that humbled him a bit. You know, he's going to be okay. **George, 1988**

Paul in *Give My Regards To Broad Street.*

I always know there's a home for me with Yoko. She's taken a lot of shit – her and Linda (McCartney). But The Beatles' breakup wasn't their fault. It was just that suddenly we were all thirty and married and changed. We couldn't carry on that life any more. From 1961, 1962, to around 1969, we were just all for each other. But suddenly you're older and you don't want to devote all that time to this one object. It was time it ended. We stopped because we'd had enough. We'd gone as far as we could with each other. And I'm sorry, but I'm not here to recreate anybody's past. The Beatles finished in 1970. It's not the main force of my life any more. Let's do the gig of today, not of yesterday. **Ringo, April 1981**

People always latch on to the first image and refuse to let go. It was the same with John. Because he had this rapier wit, they said he was nasty and things like that. But John was the kindest person I ever knew. He was the only one of the four of us who would give his soul. The three of us would hesitate, but John would give you anything without hesitation. And I loved the man dearly. We were friends all of the time.

   I love the other two, you know. We're friends, and there's no real problem, but we have arguments and little fights. We did when we were touring, and we do now. But nothing like the newspapers make it out to be. **Ringo, April 1981**

On John's Murder: And then the asshole appeared. There's no understanding it. You think about it, but I'm telling you, you never understand it. The world has lost a wonderful man. **Ringo, April 1981**

In spite of all the things, The Beatles really could play music together when they weren't uptight. And if I get a thing going Ringo knows where to go, just like that, and he does well. We've played together so long that it fits. The only thing I sometimes miss is being able to just sort of blink or make a certain noise and know they'll all know where we are going on an ad-lib thing. But I don't miss it that much. **John, 1970**

None of us are technical musicians. None of us could read music. None of us can write it. But as pure musicians, as inspired humans to make the noise, (Paul, George and Ringo) are as good as anybody. **John, September 1980**

'John Lennon: Plastic Ono Band': I think it will probably scare (Paul) into doing something decent. And then he'll scare me into doing something decent and I'll scare him...like that. I think he's capable of great work, I think he will do it. I wish he wouldn't, you know, I wish nobody would, Dylan or anybody. In me heart of hearts I wish I was the only one in the world...But I can't see him doing it twice. **John, 1970**

On Paul's 'McCartney' Album: I thought Paul's was rubbish. I think he'll make a better one when he's frightened into it. But I thought that first one was just a lot of...light and whatever, you know that crap. But when I listen to the radio and I hear George's stuff coming over, well then it's pretty bloody good. It's like that, my personal tastes are very strange. **John, 1970**

John on George's Talents: George has not done his best work yet. His talents have developed over the years and he was working with two fucking brilliant songwriters, and he learned a lot from us. I wouldn't have minded being George, the invisible man, and learning what he learned. Maybe it was hard for him sometimes, because Paul and I are such egomaniacs, but that's the game. **John, 1970**

George's relationship (with me) was one of young follower and older guy. He's three or four years younger than me. It's a love-hate relationship and I think George still bears resentment toward me for being a daddy who left home...I don't want to be that egomaniacal, but he was like a disciple of mine when we started. **John, September 1980**

I was hurt by George's book, *I, Me, Mine* – so this message will go to him. He put a book out privately on his life that, by glaring omission, says that my influence on his life is absolutely zilch and nil. In his book, which is purportedly this clarity of vision of his influence on each song he wrote, he remembers every two-bit sax player or guitarist he met in subsequent years. I'm not in the book. **John, September 1980**

George Touring in 1974: It wasn't the greatest thing in history. The guy went through some kind of mill. It was probably his turn to get smacked. When we were all together there was periods when The Beatles were in, The Beatles were out, whatever opinion people hold. There's a sort of illusion about it. But the actual fact was The Beatles were in for eight months, The Beatles were out for eight months. The public, including the media, are sometimes a bit sheeplike and if the ball starts rolling, well, it's just that somebody's in, somebody's out. George is out for the moment. And I think it didn't matter what he did on tour. **John, June 1975**

'Band on the Run' is a great album. Wings is almost as conceptual a group as Plastic Ono Band. Plastic Ono was a conceptual group, meaning that whoever was playing was the band. And Wings keeps changing all the time. It's conceptual, I mean, they're back-up men for Paul. It doesn't matter who's playing. You can call them Wings, but it's Paul McCartney music. And it's good stuff. It's good Paul music. **John, June 1975**

Paul and Linda with Wings, 1973.

I think Ringo's drumming is underrated the same way Paul's bass playing is underrated. Paul was one of the most innovative bass players ever. And half the stuff that is going on now is directly ripped off from his Beatles period. **John, September 1980**

'**The walrus is Paul**': That line was a joke, you know. That line was put in partly because I was with Yoko, and I knew I was finally high and dry. In a perverse way, I was sort of saying to Paul, "Here, have this crumb, have this illusion, have this stroke – because I'm leaving you." **John, September 1980**

I kind of admire the way Paul started back from scratch, forming a new band and playing in small dance halls, because that's what he wanted to do with The Beatles – he wanted us to go back to the dance halls and experience that again. **John, September 1980**

Ringo with his All Starr Band, 1989.

"Come Together"

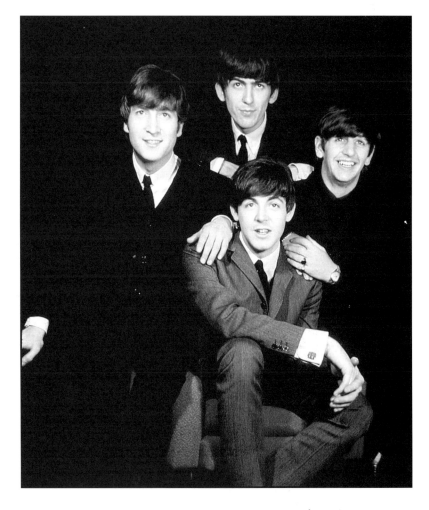

If someone were crazy enough to put up $50 million and the others were willing...The four of us are so tied up with our own lives and life goes so fast. It's not beyond the bounds of possibility, but we'd have to want to do it for the music's sake first. George, 1975

People keep on saying, "When are you getting back together again?" They don't realise I can't. There was a play on in the West End (London's Theatre District) called *John, Paul, George, Ringo & Bert*...which made out that all the others wanted to keep it going...It set me down in history as the one who broke the group up. The opposite is true. Ringo left first because he didn't think he was drumming well enough, and we persuaded him he was the best. Then George left during 'Let It Be'. They had all left. **Paul, 1984**

Through all that kind of bitterness I tended to think like John a bit, "Oh, The Beatles...naww...Crap." But it really wasn't. I think it was great. So I'd like to see that cooled out and restored to its former greatness, agree that it was a good thing and continue in some kind of way. I don't see getting The Beatles back together – there's certain things we could do quite nicely and still produce some kind of ongoing thing. I don't think you'll ever get anyone to give up all their individual stuff now; everyone's got it going too well now. **Paul, January 1974**

On Collaborating Together, After the Positive Example of All Contributing to Ringo's Album, 'Ringo' (1973): I think that's the beginning; ('Ringo') shows what someone can do just if he asks. That's all (Ringo) did. He just asked us all. So that's what I like, that no one says "Naw, you go on and make your own album." So if it's that easy then lots of things could be done in the future. And I'd like to see some great things done. **Paul, January 1974**

Paul and Ringo at the *Give My Regards To Broad Street* party.

Paul on Playing Again With John: I could. It's totally fresh ground, right now, 'cause I just got my visa, too. About two or three days ago; and until then, I couldn't physically write a song with John; he was in America. He couldn't get out. I couldn't get in. But now that's changed so whole new possibilities are opening up. Anything could happen. I like to write with John. I like to write with anyone who's good. **Paul, January 1974**

We're friends, old pals. It was only logical that we'd eventually get together again. But it's too early to say whether we'll work together. We would never be permanently together, but there might well be ventures we could reassemble for again. I wouldn't rule it out. None of us are enemies by a long shot. **Paul, 1976**

On Being Offered Millions for One Concert Reunion: Maybe in America one night we'll all loon down to a studio. I'm just playing it by ear. The main thing about this huge offer...THE HUGE OFFER...well the man's an embarrassment (American Promoter Bob Arum)...The trouble is I've always been so proud of The Beatles and the embarrassment of the thing is that so much money is being offered, most people in the world would say, "You have to accept." But I wouldn't want it that way...For me, the only way The Beatles could come back together again would be if we wanted to do something musically, not lukewarm just for the money. **Paul, 1976**

I tell you, before this tour (Wings Over America), I was tempted to ring everyone up and say, "Look, is it true we're not going to get back together, 'cause we all pretty much feel like we're not." And as long as I could get everyone to say, "No, we're definitely not," then I could say, "It's a definite no-no." But I know my feeling, and I think the others' feeling in a way, is we don't want to close the door to anything in the future. We might like it someday. **Paul, 1976**

We're on better terms yeah, but no one would pick up the group thing again...nobody wanted to work with each other. There were moments when we thought, "Ah, it would be great," but we thought if we did it, it would be a let-down; one of the things we'd always been very conscious of with The Beatles was to have a great career and leave 'em laughing. So we thought we had done that; we didn't really want to come back as decrepit old rockers. **Paul, 1982**

Getting Together With George and Ringo: I'd like to. But it's a touchy affair. I think all of us, rather than get the world's press on our backs, would rather play that aspect down for now. But I'd like to. And I know George and I have talked once or twice about maybe just plonking a couple of acoustics together. So that whole scene is warming up a bit, which is true. It's such a breath of fresh air – and it's been a long time coming, you know? **Paul, January 1986**

Playing Together for a Movie Called 'The Long and Winding Road': It was always a slight possibility, but we never really got to the point where the four of us knew of it as a concrete possibility. I think (John) thought, "Well, I might do it." I know the three of them did play together once, maybe on

(Harry Nilsson's) 'Pussy Cats'. They jammed together, and I remember, I think it was John who said to me, "Man, it was great, we're a great band." Because that's the great thing about The Beatles: we really were a great band. I mean, really. I know now from playing with other people that it's not always you can sit down and actually get in a groove. With The Beatles, it nearly always was...and that is something you cannot buy.
Paul, November 1987

Yes, we will work together again. I think that we will just meet and decide to do one or two things together, and it will grow from there. There is no hurry. We split in 1970 because we all grew up. When we split, it was like getting out of the army for all of us. We always said we would not stagger on until we were ninety, and I think the split finally came because The Beatles, as they were then, had come to an end.

Even now, I can't ever see us walking on to a stage again and singing our old numbers. But there are other things we can do together – and we will.
Paul, 1974

Jamming Unexpectedly With George and Ringo at Eric Clapton's Wedding in 1979: No, it didn't feel strange at all. We were having a booze-up and a laugh and suddenly we were playing together again. It felt pretty good to me...Oh, yeah, it'll be great to do one like that again with just the four of us, once Sean (John's son) is five and John starts playing again. **Paul, 1979**

I'd like to play with the other guys. But only for music. Just quietly some time...You never know, The Beatles might feel like getting back together again. But I mean, we'd do it very privately. If we were ever to do it, we'd just have to record some tracks, really.

But the three guys – the other two guys and myself – you think of it, we are the basic rhythm section. It's there: bass, drums and guitar. So it's interesting that it still exists.

If things loosen up, we might play together again. I'm in no hurry, but I'd like it. They're good guys, you know. I like them. Obviously you drift apart, with George into films, Ringo into this and that, doing stuff. But it would be nice. It would be fun. I think we've got to leave it there.
Paul, November 1987

Having played with other musicians I don't even think The Beatles were that good. It's all a fantasy, this idea of putting The Beatles back together again. The only way it will happen is if we're all broke. Even then I wouldn't relish playing with Paul. He's a fine bass player but he's sometimes overpowering. Ringo's got the best backbeat in the business – I'd join a band with John Lennon any day. But I wouldn't join a band with Paul McCartney. That's not personal; it's from a musician's point of view. Anyway, we're all enjoying being individuals. We'd all been boxed in for ten years. The biggest break in my career was getting in The Beatles in 1963. The second biggest break since then is getting out of them. **George, 1973**

Ringo and George at the
Prince's Trust Concert.

I have a problem, I must admit, when people try to get The Beatles together.
They're still suggesting it, even though John is dead. They still come and say,
"Why don't The Beatles get together?" Well, The Beatles can't. I suppose the
three of us could, but it was such a struggle to find our own individual
identities after The Beatles...If somebody asks me to do something, and then
next thing I find out is they've also asked Paul and Ringo, I hate...I don't
want to be set up, put into a situation where I'm tricked into being in The
Beatles again. If I'm going to be in them, I'd like to know up front.
George, November 1987

On Getting Back Together: The silliness goes on without us.
Ringo, January 1974

John's Death and the Rumours of a Beatle Reunion: You know, a sixteen-
year-old kid in the Miami airport said, "Well, at least the rumours that you're
getting together will stop now." That blew me away! But the kid was right.
I'm sorry that's what it took. I mean, I never wanted it to go to that extreme
for the rumours to stop. But of course they probably never will. There's
already all this crap going down about us doing a memorial album for John.
It's like all that get-together stuff. It's silly, you know? It used to drive us
mad. Some smartass would sprout that he's got this idea to get us together,
and it would be international news. They'd fetch up the most extreme
reasons. For the Queen of England. Well, sorry about the Queen! For the
boat people. Sorry for the boat people! But it doesn't matter how many times
we deny it, it'll still go on. Anyone who wants to be a little hero or make a
small name for himself can say he's getting us together, and he'll get an hour-
long show on TV. Even if there's only one of us left, they'll say he's getting
together with himself. **Ringo, April 1981**

Going back to The Beatles would be like going back to school. I was never one for reunions. It's all over. **John, 1971**

On Writing Songs Together for Ringo's 'Ringo' Album: I really liked the album. And I really enjoyed working with George and Ringo again. Unfortunately, Paul could not come out to the States to work on the record because he could not get a visa. But I think that we will play together again. **John, 1974**

George, Ringo, Yoko, Sean Lennon and Julian Lennon at the Rock'n'Roll Hall of Fame Awards, 1986.

The Beatles don't exist and can never exist again. John Lennon, Paul McCartney, George Harrison and Richard Starkey could put on a concert – but it can never be The Beatles singing 'Strawberry Fields' or 'I Am The Walrus' again, because we are not in our 20s. We cannot be that again, nor can the people who are listening. **John, September 1980**

When a radio station has a Beatles weekend, they usually play the same ten songs – 'A Hard Day's Night', 'Help!', 'Yesterday', 'Something', 'Let It Be' – you know, there's all that wealth of material, but we hear only ten songs. So the deejay says, "I want to thank John, Paul, George and Ringo for not getting back together and spoiling a good thing." I thought it was a good sign. Maybe people are catching on. **John, September 1980**

If The Beatles or the Sixties had a message, it was learn to swim. Period. And once you learn to swim, swim. The people who are hung up on The Beatles' and Sixties' dream missed the whole point when The Beatles' and the Sixties' dream became the point.

Carrying The Beatles' or the Sixties' dream around all your life is like carrying the Second World War and Glenn Miller around. That's not to say you can't enjoy Glenn Miller or The Beatles, but to live in that dream is the twilight zone. It's not living now. It's an illusion. **John, September 1980**

BIBLIOGRAPHY

Books:

John Blake, *All You Needed Was Love: The Beatles After The Beatles*, Perigee Books, New York 1981.

Peter Brown and Steven Gaines, *The Love You Make: An Insider's Story of The Beatles*, Pan Books, London 1984.

Chet Flippo, *McCartney: The Biography*, Fontana Paperbacks, London 1989.

Goldie Friede, Robin Titone and Sue Weiner, *The Beatles A To Z*, Methuen, New York 1980.

Geoffrey Giuliano, *Dark Horse: The Secret Life of George Harrison*, Bloomsbury Publishing Ltd., London 1989.

George Harrison, *I, Me, Mine*, W. H. Allen, London 1982.

Paul McCartney, *The Paul McCartney World Tour*, Concert Programme, London 1990.

Ross Michaels, *George Harrison Yesterday & Today*, Quick Fox Publishers, New York 1977.

Andy Peebles, *The Lennon Tapes*, BBC Publications, London 1980.

John Robertson, *The Art & Music of Lennon*, Omnibus Press, London 1990.

The Editors of Rolling Stone, *The Ballad of John & Yoko*, Rolling Stone Press, New York 1982.

Geoffrey Stokes, *The Beatles*, Omnibus Press, London 1981.

Chris Welch, *Paul McCartney: The Definitive Biography*, Proteus Books, London 1984.

Jan Wenner, *Lennon Remembers*, Popular Library, New York 1971.

Bob Woffinden, *The Beatles Apart*, Proteus Books, London 1981.

Magazines & Newspapers:

Playboy Magazine, Chicago.

Rolling Stone, New York.

Q Magazine, London.

New Musical Express, London.

The Independent, London.